THE ATLANTIC CRITICAL STUDIES

WILLIAM SHAKESPEARE'S
Antony and Cleopatra

THE ATLANTIC CRITICAL STUDIES

WILLIAM SHAKESPEARE'S
Antony and Cleopatra

RATRI RAY

ATLANTIC
PUBLISHERS & DISTRIBUTORS (P) LTD

Published by

ATLANTIC

PUBLISHERS & DISTRIBUTORS (P) LTD

7/22, Ansari Road, Darya Ganj, New Delhi-110002
Phones : +91-11-40775252, 23273880, 23275880, 23280451
Fax : +91-11-23285873
Web : www.atlanticbooks.com
E-mail : orders@atlanticbooks.com

Branch Office
5, Nallathambi Street, Wallajah Road, Chennai-600002
Phones : +91-44-64611085, 32413319
E-mail : chennai@atlanticbooks.com

Printed in India at Nice Printing Press, A-33/3A, Site-IV, Industrial Area, Sahibabad, Ghaziabad, U.P.

General Preface

The Atlantic Critical Studies are modelled on the study-aids available in England and America, among other places, and are primarily meant for the students of English Literature of Indian universities.

However, in consideration of the local conditions and the various constraints under which our students have to study—non-availability of relevant critical books, dearth of foreign and Indian journals, inaccessibility to good, well-equipped libraries, just to mention a few of them—the models have been considerably improved upon, both qualitatively and quantitatively.

Thus, while these studies are meant to be comprehensive and self-sufficient, the distinguished scholars who have prepared these study materials, have taken special care to combine lucidity and profundity in their treatment of the texts.

The Select Bibliography at the end, or References in the chapters are meant not only to acknowledge the sources used but also to help a student in the pursuit of further studies if he/she wants to.

Atlantic Publishers & Distributors (P) Ltd. believe in quality and excellence. These studies will only reconfirm it.

MOHIT K. RAY

Chief Editor [English Literature]

Atlantic Publishers & Distributors (P) Ltd.,

New Delhi

Introduction

The Golden Age of English Literature, the Elizabethan Age, produced a veritable host of outstanding literary talents, but there can be no doubt that the brightest star in this galaxy was William Shakespeare. His was a genius that expressed itself primarily through the medium of drama, but he had also written memorable narrative poems, and his sonnet-sequence stands unrivalled in its complexity of feeling and felicity of expression even now.

There is great range and variety in the plays he had written, as he had not left any of the kinds of drama unexplored. Not every dramatist of his age had tried his hand at tragedy, comedy and chronicle plays and succeeded in each. His greatest rival Christopher Marlowe, for example, wrote only tragedies and Ben Jonson was successful only in his satirical comedies. Within these three main genres, again, there is more variety in Shakespeare than in any other dramatist. His tragedies, for example, range from Scotland to Egypt as far as space is concerned, and all the four main kinds of Elizabethan tragedy of blood can be found in his works. Thus we have the conqueror tragedy in *Macbeth*, the revenge tragedy in *Hamlet,* the domestic tragedy in *Romeo and Juliet,* and the villain tragedy in *Othello*. These labels, however, can by no means do justice to the rich complexity of these plays. Among comedies too there is a similar variety. *Twelfth Night* is a romantic comedy and *As You Like It* is a pastoral comedy. *Measure for Measure* is a problem comedy and *The Tempest* is a romance. Again, these classifications are all tentative ones. As far as the chronicle plays are concerned, he wrote about English history as well as Roman history. The latter can be called historical tragedies and are usually referred to as the Roman tragedies. In every instance he took up a popular kind of play and then developed it in such a manner that it suffered "a sea-change / Into something rich and strange", to use his own words (*The Tempest*).

Like most of the dramatists of his time, Shakespeare took the material of his plays from different sources, like pre-existing plays, popular stories, etc. His treatment of this diverse material is a proof of his great organizing capacity and his unfailing artistic instinct. He condensed stories that were too long, omitted irrelevant material and expanded stage-worthy episodes. Such alterations were made with an unerring judgement which made the play successful on the stage and turned it into a work that defied time and space and became universal.

Antony and Cleopatra is the product of his mature artistry. It belongs to the group of the Roman plays. It is both a history and a tragedy. There are three plays written in this group, *Julius Caesar, Antony and Cleopatra* and *Coriolanus*. There are other plays dealing with Roman characters, but they do not come within this group. *Titus Andronicus* is a Senecan tragedy and *Timon of Athens* a problem comedy. *Antony and Cleopatra* is a play faithful to history, for Shakespeare had followed the Roman historian, Plutarch very closely. Yet it is not just a history play, as will be seen when the topic of its genre is discussed.

Every aspect of his plays has intrigued and inspired scholars and critics. Everyone, however, agrees about one thing– Shakespeare's greatness as a dramatist. Critics–from his great contemporary, Ben Jonson onwards–have been unanimous on this one subject. Dr. Johnson, perhaps, expresses it the best:

> The work of a correct and regular writer is a garden accurately formed and diligently planted, varied with shades, and scented with flowers; the composition of Shakespeare is a forest, in which oaks extend their branches, and pines tower in the air, interspread sometimes with weeds and brambles.[1]

RATRI RAY

NOTE

1. F. Brady and W.K. Wimsatt. *Samuel Johnson: Selected Poetry and Prose*. University of California Press, 1977, p. 316.

Contents

General Preface .... *v*

Introduction .... *vii*

1. The Background 1
2. Life and Works 11
3. The Story and the Genre 34
4. A Scene-wise Analysis of the Play 48
5. The Major Themes 84
6. The Major Characters 99
7. The Minor Characters 122
8. The Plot-Structure 141
9. Imagery in *AC* 162
10. Poetic Style: Diction and Versification 174
11. Critical Reception: A Brief History 188

1

The Background

(A) THE SOCIO-POLITICAL BACKGROUND

No, creative artist can be truly appreciated unless a knowledge of his socio-political as well as literary perspective can be obtained. We all are, as Arnold had observed, parts of a single continent. A sketchy knowledge of Shakespeare's background is, therefore, necessary in order to understand his drama. A chronological table of some of the important socio-political events of his time is given below, to be followed by a few explanatory remarks. Religion was one of the important issues of his time and so the main religious events are mentioned as well as the main scientific events. It was a time of geographical expansion as well as of military exploits. A study of this table will give a more or less comprehensive picture of the overall background of the age.

A Chronological Table

1558 — Queen Mary I dies. Elizabeth I succeeds.

— Mary Queen of Scots marries the French Dauphin.

'59 — Mary Queen of Scots declares herself Queen of England, though Elizabeth I is the Queen.

— War between Spain and France ends.

— Church of England established.

'60 — Scottish Parliament establishes the Reformed Church and breaks with Rome.

'61 — Mary Queen of Scots returns from France. She *clashes* with the Calvinists.

'62 — The Huguenots start emigrating from France to England.

'63 — Bubonic plague epidemic starts.

'64 — *Shakespeare born.* Anglo-French war ends. England at war with Spain. The Thirty-nine Articles adopted by the Church of England. Queen Elizabeth tries to enforce uniformity.

'67 — Mary Queen of Scots abdicates. Rugby School founded.

'68 — Mary Queen of Scots flees to England and is held captive by Queen Elizabeth.

'69 — Rebellion of the Roman Catholic earls crushed.

'70 — Pope Pius V excommunicates Queen Elizabeth.

'74 — Burbage gets licence for the first theatre in London.

'76 — Tycho Brahe begins his astronomical observations.

— Burbage opens the first theatre in London.

'77 — Treaty with the Dutch. Drake begins his circumnavigation of the world.

'80 — Drake completes his circumnavigation.

'81 — Conversion to Catholicism is declared treasonable.

— Galileos Law of the Pendulum.

'83 — Plot against the Queen. Humphrey Gilbert takes possession of Newfoundland in the name of the Queen.

'84 — Ralaeigh discovers and names Virginia after the Queen. He starts to colonize it.

'86 — England wins the Battle of Zutphen in which Sir Philip Sidney dies.

— Plot against the Queen. Mary Queen of Scots implicated and convicted of treason.

'87 — Rose Theatre built by Henslowe.

'88 — Defeat of the Spanish Armada.

'89 — Galileo publishes the results of his experiments with falling bodies.

'92 — John Davis discovers the Falkland islands.

'93 — Absence from the church on Sundays made punishable by law.

'95 — Southwell, RC priest and mystical poet executed after three years imprisonment for celebrating Mass.

'96 — England, France and Netherlands form alliance against Spain. Peasants rebel in Oxfordshire.

'97 — Irish Rebellion. Statutory Provision for Poor Relief. Beggary made illegal. Convicts transported to colonies.

'98 — The Bodleian Library begun. Globe theatre opened.

1603 — Queen Elizabeth dies. Accession of King James I.

'04 — Peace with Spain. Gunpowder Plot is made.

— Acts against priests and recusants. Anglican canons made. Silk manufacture begins.

'05 — Gunpowder Plot discovered. Repression of Puritans and Catholics. Colonists land in Barbados.

'08 — Failure of plan for union with Scotland. Microscope and telescope invented in Netherlands.

'01 — Judicial decision against royal proclamations. Old Testament for English Roman Catholics published.

'11 — Parliament dissolved.

'12 — Alliance with German Protestant princes. Last recorded execution for heresy. First tobacco plantation in Virginia. Bermuda colonized.

'16 — *Shakespeare dies.*

It can be readily inferred from this table that the throne of England was anything but secure in the beginning. There was continuous warfare with the neighbouring nations and plots against the Queen at home. It took Queen Elizabeth quite a few years to make her seat secure on the throne. She brought security in the country and, because of her tolerant religious policy, put an end to religious controversies. An observant contemporary has called her "a shrewd, learned and moderate young woman". England was able to reach, gradually but with finality, a compromise in the matter of religion. G.M. Trevelyan says:

> In the year in which the Queen succeeded her sister Mary, Puritanism was mainly a foreign doctrine imported from Geneva and Rhineland; when she died it was rootedly and characteristically English. ...Anglicanism had also taken root and shape in the Queen's reign.[1]

Queen Elizabeth's most serious rival, Mary Queen of the Scots had strong support. So it took the Queen some time before she could be secure on the throne. Towards the end of her reign the question of succession became a vexatious one, but during her reign her tolerance and wisdom brought security and prosperity to England.

England was expanding in all directions. Socially speaking, the class barriers existed but it was a thing generally accepted. Moreover, there was no oppression of the lower classes by the feudal lords. G.M. Trevelyan points out:

> Class divisions in Shakespeare's day were taken as a matter of course, without jealous'y in those below, or itching anxiety on the part of the upper and middle classes.[2]

Everyone earned his living by honest labour and this fact fostered self-respect in everyone. Mine host of Tabard Inn was fully worthy of respect from those who visited his hostelry, from the Knight to the Miller.

But no one denied the existence of the poor. The Poor Law showed the awareness of social duty by providing for the unemployed and the destitute. Law and order was in the hands of influential local lords who functioned as the Queen's Justices of the Peace to settle minor local disputes and cases of lawbreaking. These J.P.S. were themselves under the jurisdiction of the Privy Council.

Industrial prosperity went on increasing because of the factory system which came to be introduced at this time. Mining too was extended in every field so that not only did coal become available to all but so did metals like tin, iron, lead and copper. The kettle could sing over a coal fire in every house.

Sir Francis Drake enhanced the national pride by his two remarkable achievements—the circumnavigation of the world and defeating the Spanish Armada. This is repeatedly referred to in the Literature of the mid-Elizabethan period. The age saw expansion in every direction, along with great prosperity and security.

> By the end of Elizabeth's reign not only was England commercially and financially thus reviving and expanding on a modern basis but her ancient rivals were in rapid decline.[3]

The reign of King James I or the Jacobean Age continued the expansion and prosperity. London continued to grow and trade expanded. Not many significant changes took place in the next forty years. No industrial or agricultural changes were there, though there were changes enough in the political sphere. The accession of King James brought about the union of the royal houses of England and Scotland, but, in spite of much trying the two kingdoms remained separate from each other. Paradoxically, Holland was more important from the social-cultural viewpoint than Scotland. Shakespeare's Dark Lady is thought to have been a Flemish beauty.

The Jacobean Age saw the beginnings of colonization. The signing of the peace treaty with Spain (1604) removed all threats from the ocean, so settlers from England moved to newly-acquired foreign lands of New England, Virginia, etc. The seeds of the British Empire were being sown. Religious as well as commercial motives were impelling these settlers to brave the seas. Tempests and shipwrecks were frequent and one of them formed the first scene of the *The Tempest*. But these are of interest only to the historians. What mattered to our poet was the audience, "the many-tongu'd beast":

> ...they were eager for plot and pageant, noise and knock-about, ...and learned wit and music of the best.... He accepted the tradition, and in twenty more years, expanded it into something far greater than the most consummate of public entertainments.[4]

(B) THE LITERARY BACKGROUND

Shelley's famous Lines inp *Hellas* "The world's great age begins anew. The golden years return" could easily have been written about the Elizabethan Age. It was not only drama that was developing, but the other literary forms too were undergoing a renewal of life and startling development. A chronological table is being given that covers the main literary events of the time, including the births and deaths of prominent literary figures. This will be followed by more details. The table begins with the first performance of *Ralph Roister Doister* which took place ten years before Shakespeare was born, and the year Sir Philip Sidney was born. The plays of Shakespeare have not been mentioned here as they will be dealt with later. (Chapter 2 Infra)

A Chronological Table

1554 — Sir Philip Sidney and Lyly born. *Ralph Roister Doister* staged.

'57 — Tottel's *Miscellany*. North *The Dial of Princes.*

'58 — Lodge, Kyd, Greene, Peele born.

'61 — *Gorboduc* performed. Bacon born.

'63 — Drayton and Donne born.

'64 — Shakespeare and Marlowe born.

'66 — Gascoigne's *Supposes.* Painter's *Palace of Pleasure.*

'67 — Campion and Nashe born.

'75 — Heywood and Tourneur born.

'76 — *Paradyse of Daynty Devises.*

'77 — Holinshed's *Chronicles.*

'79 — Spenser's *Shepherd's Calendar. Schole of Abuse.*

'85 — Kyd's *Spanish Tragedy.*

'86 — Sir Philip Sidney dies. Lyly's *Endimion.*

'87 — *Tamburlaine, Gallathea* (Lyly). *The Misfortunes of Arthur.*

'89 — Marlowe's *The Jew of Malta. The Arte of English Poesie.*

'90 — *The Faerie Queene* Bks I-III, Sidney's *Arcadia.*

'91 — *Astrophel and Stella. Old Wives' Tale. Edward II.*

'92 — Revised *Arcadia,* Daniel's sonnet-sequence *To Delia, Arden of Feversham. Hero and Leander* (Marlowe).

'95 — *Amoretti, Epithalamion, Apology for Poetry.*

'99 — Spenser dies. *Every Man Out of His Humour.*

1600 — *England's Helicon, England's Parnassus, Cynthia's Revels* (Ben Jonson).

'01 — Dekker and Marston's *Satiromastix. Poetaster.*

'03 — Downland's *Third Book of Songs, A Woman Killed with Kindness.* Jonson's *Sejanus.*

'04 — *Bussy D'Ambois,* Marston's Malcontent.

'05 — Bacon's *Advancement of Learning.* Eastward Ho! Middleton's *A Trick to Catch the Old One.*

'06 — Lyly dies. *Yorkshire Tragedy. Volpone. Revenger's Tragedy.*

'07 — Beaumont and Fletcher's *Knight of the Burning Pestle.*

'08 — Fuller and Milton born. Fletcher's *The Faithful Shepherdess.*

'09 — *Philaster.* Fulke Greville's *Mustapha.*

'10 — Jonson's *The Alchemist.*

'11 — Spenser's *Collected Works. The Authorised Version of the Bible. A King and No King.*

'12 — Crashaw born. Chapmans *Iliad* I-XXIV. *The White Devil* by Webster. Drayton's *Poly-Olbion.*

'14 — Constable and Overbury die. Purchas' *Pilgrimage.* Sir Walter Raleigh's *History of the World.* Ben Jonson's *Bartholomew Fair. Duchess of Malfi.*

'16 — Shakespeare dies. Jonson given royal pension Chapman's *Whole Works of Homer. Jonson Works,* his *The Devil is an Ass.*

These six decades can be said to cover the best time of literary efflorescence in England. Sir Philip Sidney did not live to see it, the names that we are familiar with come much later than him. He saw the bud, not the full-blown rose in its glory.

The beginnings of drama can be traced from this time, for Sidney saw *Gorboduc* staged and wrote:

> [It] is full of stately speeches and well sounding phrases, climbing to the heights of Seneca's style and as full of notable morality which it doth most delightfully teach and so obtain the very end of poesy.[5]

After this the state of drama improved by leaps and bounds. Many plays were being written and staged during our poet's childhood, all of which were of an inferior kind. It was the childhood of Renaissance drama. A year after Sidney's death *Tamburlaine* was to be performed by the only poet who could have been a serious rival of Shakespeare had he lived.

By the time Shakespeare started writing he already had many pre-existing models to follow and improve upon, not only in drama but in other literary forms also, e.g. sonnets, songs, narrative poems, etc. The scenery here in early Elizabethan Age was but marginally better than that in drama. Spenser's *Shepheardes Calendar* and the first few books of *Faerie Queene* before our poet's debut with *Venus and Adonis*. Tottel's *Miscellany* published the sonnets of Wyatt and Surrey but it was only in the last decade of the century that the famous sequences were written. "The Elizabethan nest of singing birds" started writing mostly from 1580 onwards and kept it up till 1620. The poets were mostly anonymous and the songs were published in many anthologies with inspiring names: *Paradyse of Daynty Devises* and *England's Helicon* being two such. Analysing the features of these songs Yvor Winters says:

> Only a master of style can deal successfully in a plain manner with obvious matter: we are concerned with the type of poetry which is perhaps the hardest to compose and the last to be recognized, a poetry not striking nor original as to subject, but merely true and universal.[6]

The Elizabethan Age, in its triumphal progress, showed a breathtaking wealth of many kinds of poems: narrative, lyrical, discursive, religious, etc. Prose too did not lag behind. Writers like Lord Bacon, Sir Thomas Browne, Burton, Hooker and many others were there to develop and polish it.

For the purposes of this study, it is drama that is of interest. In tragedy, which is the form of peculiar interest to us, the prevailing influence was that of Seneca. Kyd's famous *The Spanish Tragedy,* a revenge tragedy to lead all later such plays, was in the Senecan mode. *Tamburlaine* by Marlowe rivalled it in popularity. Burbage first and then Henslowe established theatre halls that staged plays regularly and were the chief sources of entertainment. One after the other, the great dramatists experimented with different kinds of plays and honed their dramatic skills to a keen edge. There were tragedies of four different kinds, comedies catering to all the different classes in society, history plays and farces coming forth in an endless stream. The late Elizabethan Age produced many dramatists of great talent though the highest peak was reached in the Jacobean Age. Besides our own poet there were the University Wits, Ben Jonson, Webster, Chapman, Tourneur, Marston, Dekker, Heywood, Beaumont and Fletcher and many such.

The tragedies following Seneca have been designated as the Tragedy of Blood and divided into four categories. Conqueror tragedies centred around a highly ambitious person, like those of Marlowe. The Revenge tragedy was started by Kyd and was a highly popular one. The Villain tragedy was the third kind, Middleton and Rowley's *The Changeling* being one of the best examples. The fourth kind of tragedy was the domestic tragedy. *The Yorkshire Tragedy* and *Arden of Feversham*, both anonymous, are the best examples of this kind of play. Our poet, needless to say, excelled in all four and added to each of them so significantly that his own plays soar far beyond the limitations of labels.

Another kind of play, which is of special interest in the present instance, was the chronicle play or the history play. Some of these plays, as they end with the death of the hero, can be called historical tragedy. Marlowe's *Edward II* is one such, and, indeed, the play under discussion, *Antony and Cleopatra* is one. Apart from a few such plays that are definitely tragic, the chronicle play, with its pageant of historical figures, usually stands free of any such designation as tragedy and comedy. Shakespeare's own history plays do so.

The masque was another form of entertainment. They were used for celebrating happy occasions like betrothals, marriages, etc. The masque celebrating the betrothal of Ferdinand and Miranda in *The Tempest*, the one in *As You Like It* are examples of masques. Ben Jonson wrote many of them.

Then there were farces, providing boisterous clowning and laughter. Though Shakespeare did not favour this form much, even he wrote one, at the special request of the Queen herself. She had been enchanted by Falstaff and wanted to see "the fat knight in love". So *The Merry Wives of Windson* was written. It is the only farce he wrote.

Shakespeare's England thus showed a fine burgeoning and flourishing of diverse elements. Specially the form of drama reached heights to be barely equalled since then. F.P. Wilson has stressed the active contribution of the audience and the actors in this respect:

> With such an audience and such actors a drama was possible that was neither coterie art nor sheer vulgarity and rant, but one that was fed by a wide range of interests.... *Mutatis mutandis,* this will do to suggest the different levels at which Shakespeare's plays have appealed from his day to ours.[7]

REFERENCES

1. Trevelyan, G.M. *Illustrated English Social History*, Vol. 2. Harmondsworth, Penguin Books Ltd., p. 125.
2. *Ibid.*, p. 61.
3. *Ibid.*, p. 123.
4. *Ibid.*, pp. 128-29.
5. Sir Philip Sidney. *An Apology for Poetry* in Enright, D.J. and Chickera E. eds. *English Critical Texts,* Oxford, OUP. 21st Impression, 2002, p. 4.
6. Winters, Y. *The Sixteenth Century Lyric in England* in Alpers, P.J. ed., *Elizabethan Poetry*. Oxford, OUP, 1967, p. 96.
7. Wilson, F.P. *Elizabethan and Jacobean Drama* in Kaufmann, R.J. ed., *Elizabethan Drama,* Oxford, OUP, 1961, p. 5.

2

Life and Works

(A) A SHORT BIOGRAPHY

Considering the fact that the Elizabethan Age produced so much literature of such high calibre it is surprising how little is known about the geniuses who produced them. Very little, for example, is known about Ben Jenson or Webster. Shakespeare from this point of view is very rewarding. This is a significant fact in itself and is due largely to the social status of his family and the respect in which it was held. A.L. Rowse has most pertinently observed.

> We are fortunate to know as much as we do about the early years of Shakespeare.... The Shakespeare lay thick on the ground in those villages north of the river....[1]

Apart from this there is the fact that he himself was a well-known and well-loved figure. He had, in fact, become an almost legendary figure in his lifetime itself. Not only facts and figures, but legends also accumulated around and about his august name. Irving Ribner, pointing out this fact, has also explained it:

> As a dramatist, Shakespeare acquired considerable reputation during his own lifetime. It continued to grow in the centuries following his death in 1616, accumulating as it did an accretion of legends and anecdotes.[2]

First of all, a chronological table of the important events of his life is being given below.

A Chronological Table of the Chief Events of His Life

1564 — Apr. 23, St. George's Day, supposed date of birth.
— Apr. 26, Christening ceremony performed.
'71 — Shakespeare possibly enrolled in the Grammar School.
'78 — Reversal of fortune for his father.
'82 — Marries Anne Hathaway.
'83 — Birth of Susanna, his first daughter.
'85 — The twins, Hamnet and Judith, baptised.
'86 — He leaves Stratford-upon-Avon for London.
'93 — *Venus and Adonis* published.
'94 — *Rape of Lucrece*, *Titus Andronicus* published.
'96 — Hamnet dies.
'97 — He buys New Place.
'99 — Buys shares in the Globe Theatre.
1602 —Buys 107 acre of land. Birth of first grandchild.
'04 — His company comes under Royal patronage.
'11 — Retires to Stratford.
'13 — *The Tempest* performed.
'16 — Jan. 25 – His will drawn up.
— Apr. 23 – Shakespeare dies, on his fifty-second b'day.
— Apr 25 – Buried in the chancel of Stratford church.

One of the few reliable dates we have got is that of his christening. He was baptised in the parish church of Stratford-upon-Avon and it has been recorded in the Register of Baptism in official Latin:

1564, Apr. 26, Gulielmus Filius Johannes Shakespeare[3]

With regard to the spelling of his name, it should be noted that spelling words was a very fluid process in his times. Queen Elizabeth, for example, had spelled her name in five different ways in the course of writing but one page in a document.

Since a baby was usually baptised three days after its birth the 23rd of April is usually taken to be the date of his birth, the village being Stratford-upon-Avon and the country Warwickshire.

After this the biographer does not have much concrete information to rely upon. Different biographers assign different dates to his enrolment at school, his leaving the school, going to London, etc.

Many local legends have led the writers to conclude that he had a happy and secure childhood in a thriving family. He was the third child and the first son of his parents. His father was a prosperous tradesman, dealing in gloves, corn, etc. He eventually came to be the mayor of Stratford and Alderman in 1565 and could, and did, claim the status of a gentleman. His mother, Mary Arden, came from a family a bit higher in the social scale.

One of the few details that is known of his family life at this time is that his father, being the Justice of Peace and the High Bailiff of the town, was often involved in judicial matters. Scholars have inferred that Shakespeare, being the eldest son, must have often gone with him to the law courts and thus got his knowledge of legal affairs.

Queen Elizabeth had had Grammar Schools established throughout England for the education of all boys and Shakespeare was duly admitted to the one in his village. It has become known that he was about seven years old at the time and by no means a good and eager student. Often he played truant. The subjects taught in the school were Latin grammar and literature and whatever knowledge he had of these was picked up here, where he studied till he was perhaps 14 or 16 years old.

Ben Jonson had remarked that he had but "small Latin and less Greek," but the Latin was by no means as small as it is thought to be. The school had long hours: from six in the morning till five in the evening, with a total of two and a half hours break spread out throughout the day. The curriculum, as has already been pointed out, consisted of Latin grammar and Literature. Virgil, Horace, Ovid and Mantuan had to be studied for poetry, and Caesar, Livy and Cicero in prose. Seneca, Plautus and Terence had to be studied in drama. One of his biographers, Irving Ribner, has remarked:

> Today all scholars are agreed that Shakespeare was a well-educated man of his times, that he certainly continued to further his education by wide reading throughout his life and that there was no display of learning in any one of his plays which could not have been acquired at the Stratford Grammar School.[3]

John Dover Wilson, however thinks that he did not attend the Grammar School at all. He thinks that Shakespeare's father, being a catholic, would not have put him in a school at all. Instead he might have put his son into the house of some Catholic nobleman where he would have received his education and a preliminary knowledge of acting and the lifestyle of aristocratic families.

Besides acquiring knowledge, his years at school were fruitful in other ways as well, for it was at this time that many travelling companies of players patronised by the great Earls of Leicester, Warwick and Worcester visited Stratford. They enacted not only the old native Morality plays and Interludes but the new five-Act plays modelled after the classical ones.

It is not known for sure how long he studied at the school. He was withdrawn from this school while still in his teens. A few years later one of the most important events of his life took place: he met Anne Hathaway. She was the daughter of a prosperous farmer and the belle of the entire locality. A couplet by an anonymous admirer says:

> Anne Hathaway, she hath a way
> To charm all hearts, Anne Hathaway.

She was fully eight years older than him. This age bar was not of much importance as the two got married on Nov. 28, 1582. Next year their first child Susanna was born. Nearly two years later the twins, Hamnet and Judith were born. Hamnet died in 1596.

So by the time he was 21, Shakespeare had, not only a wife eight years older than himself but three children to bring up. It was very necessary that he should set about earning a living.

A certain tradition sets it about that he taught in a school near Stratford. This detail has been handed down by John Aubrey, one of the first biographers in English. He had heard from a member of the family of one of the actors of the time who had said that Shakespeare:

> ...understood Latin pretty well for he had been in his young days a school-master in the country.[4]

There is another well-known story about how he and a few others stole a deer from the preserves of Sir Thomas Lucy at Charlecote. It is thought that Sir Thomas ordered Shakespeare to be arrested and whipped. Whether the story is true or not cannot be known for sure, but it was circulated by the actor Thomas Betterton and a contemporary clergyman. It is thought, however, that it was because of these reasons that he left Stratford in 1586.

At about this time the theatrical group named The Queen's Players visited the village and this too is supposed to have prompted him to leave the place and seek his fortunes in London.

Not only the Queen's men but other troupes also visited Stratford and Shakespeare had plenty of opportunities to become familiar with stage-performances. In 1583 alone there were three well-known groups which came there. In 1587 two famous and well-organised troupes visited Stratford which by this time had become a town. His biographers think that he had acted in the plays that had been staged. It is possible that he had been taken on as one of the actors in one of these troupes and come to London with them, though it is only a conjecture. Nothing is known for sure.

The years from 1586 to 1592 are known as the Dark Years as nothing definite is known about them. There are many legends about these first few years in London. It is said that he got a job as an assistant to the prompter in the theatre and it is also said that he eked out a living by holding the horses of the noblemen who visited the theatre. It is also thought that he renewed acquaintance with Richard Field who had been a fellow-villager and come to London a few years ago. This story is likely to be a true one since it was this Richard Field who had become a well-established printer in London and had published *Venus and Adonis* and The *Rape of Lucrece* in 1593 and 1594 respectively.

Shakespeare's arrival in London coincided with that of Marlowe. The eighties decade was a particularly stimulating one. It was at this time that Sir Francis Drake was scouring the Spanish main. Sir Philip Sidney had started to write his sonnet-sequence *Astrophel and Stella* and also his *Arcadia*. The university Wits were converging towards London and in Ireland Spenser was writing *The Faerie Queene*. Lyly had already written his *Euphues* and had turned his attention to drama. His comedies had already been staged before the Queen herself in 1584. Peele had presented his play which was very much like a modern musical comedy, *The Arraignment of Paris*. Robert Greene, Thomas Nashe and Thomas Kyd had already arrived in London. Marlowe's *Tamburlaine* was staged in 1587 and Shakespeare was definitely in London by that time. English drama as in the making at that time. F.E. Halliday has given an inspiring picture:

> Shakespeare had arrived in London at the most thrilling moment in its history; thrilling however, not only because danger, anxiety, expectation and hope were in the air, but also because the long awaited dramatic revival was imminent.[5]

The first mention of Shakespeare to be found is in a work by Greene which has, ironically enough, become famous for this reason. It is a pamphlet named *Greene's Groats worth of wit*. At the end of this there is a letter addressed to his friends, Marlowe, Peele and Nashe. He warns them not to trust actors and particularly mentions a certain actor who cannot be anyone but Shakespeare:

> Yes, trust them not: for there is an upstart crow, beautified with our feathers that with his Tyger's heart wrapt in a Player's hyde, supposes he is as well able to bombast out a blank verse as the best of you: and being an absolute Johannes factotum, is in his own conceit the only Shake-scene in a country.[6]

Greene has mockingly adopted a line from Henry IV Pt III which, together with "shake-scene" establishes the identity of the person referred to. The line in the play is "O tiger's heart wrapped in a woman's hide" which Greene has changed to "Tyger's heart wrapt in a player's hide." What is important here is that Shakespeare had, by this time, become important enough to cause jealousy in the heart of an well established university wit—no mean achievement for what, according to these men, was only a half-educated provincial.

Critics call these the years of apprenticeship, but they were highly productive as well. The sonnets were written at this time, as indeed, were the two narrative poems, *Venus and Adonis* and *Henry VI* trilogy, *Richard III, Titus Andronicus*, *The Comedy of Errors*, *The Two Gentlemen of Verona* and *The Taming of the Shrew*. The plays were highly successful on the stage. The title-page of *Titus Andronicus* (published in 1594) says in flattering terms:

> as it was played by the Rt. Hon. the Earl of Derby, the Earl of Pembroke and the Earl of Sussex their servants.[7]

This list means that the play was staged by these three well-known troupes. But more than that the list of the plays given above is significant because it means that Shakespeare, unlike Kyd and Marlowe who wrote only tragedies, could already at this early stage turn his hands to all kinds of plays: tragedy, comedy and history. Thus by 1594 he had already produced these, by which time Marlowe had already been killed. His versatility had proved itself.

By this time Shakespeare had become well-established in the group named the Lord Chamberlaine's. His name occurs along with those of Will Kempe and Burbage, both famous actors in a receipt of the Royal Treasury where all of them had been paid for producing two plays at Court. Shakespeare continued with this group till the end of his career.

It was at this time that he paid a visit to Stratford. His father was in his sixties. He himself was only twenty-eight and Susanna his eldest was nine. Hamnet was old enough to go to school. He stayed at home for four months and probably wrote *Richard III* and *Venus and Adonis* at this time. He dedicated the poem to the Earl of Southampton, the "onlie better" of the sonnet-sequence he was to write.

Henry Wriothesley the young aristocrat was not only his patron but a very intimate friend. It had been thought, because of the sonnet-sequence dedicated to him, that they present an engrossing picture of the relationship between him and the Earl in real life. The passionate love of Shakespeare for this young man has been expressed in language that can hardly be paralleled. The sonnets describe a certain Dark Lady who in a triangular love-affair had betrayed him with the Earl. It is a harrowing story that emerges from the sonnets. According to the sonnets Shakespeare loved Mr. W.H. whom the critics have identified with this Earl with an intense Petrarchan love. But he was also attracted, in spite of himself, to the Dark Lady and introduced her to Mr. W.H. (the Earl). These two then betrayed him. This painful story may or may not be true, but it is the biographer's duty to mention it, however sketchily.

Shakespeare's love for Mr. W.H. bordered on worship. Indeed, J.B. Leishman has talked about the "religiousness" of his love in the sonnets. He says in the dedication to *The Rape of Lucrece*:

> The love I dedicate to your Lordship is without end...what I have done is yours, what I have to do is yours, being part in all I have, devoted to yours.[8]

Shakespeare's life went on, climbing one peak of success after another. He bought a share in his own company and this indicates security as well as prosperity which was by no means common for all:

> It meant all the difference between the dreadful insecurity poor Greene and others had died of, and having firm ground under his feet.[9]

His company became the leading theatrical company. Before the end of the reign of Queen Elizabeth it had given thirty-two performances at the Court itself, besides public performances. He was the only dramatist to survive the destruction of the Plague. By this time Kyd, Marlowe and Greene were already dead and Peele would die in a few years. Lyly and Lodge had virtually stopped writing and Nashe had started writing pamphlets. There were no rivals. The only writer who would be his equal, Ben Jonson, would appear a few years later. His star was at its height.

The early plays now poured forth: *A Midsummer Night's Dream*, *Love's Labour's Lost*, *Romeo and Juliet* and *The Merchant of Venice*. It was 1595 and he was thirty. The first literary mention of his name is to be found now in a poem by Henry Willoughby, an Oxford undergraduate. He mentions our poet, under the initials W.S., as a mentor who gives the poet good worldly advice in matters of the heart. Then the writer gives his name as that of a poet:

> Yet Tarquin plucked his glistering grape
> And Shakespeare paints poor Lucrece's rape[10]

1597 saw the death of his only son Hamnet, at the age of eleven years. He was in Stratford at the time, writing *King John*. His father had made him renew the application at the Herald's College for the granting of a coat-of-arms. This would give the family the status of a gentleman which mattered very much in the feudal and hierarchical society of the time. This was granted and when he went back to London it was as a gentleman. He also bought New Place which was the second best house in the town.

He was such a notable figure by 1598 that Francis Meres, in his famous *Palladis Tamia* referred to him in a reverential manner, comparing him with the classical poets, listing his plays:

> ...the sweet wittie soule of Ovid lives in mellifluous and honey-tongu'd Shakespeare, witness his Venus and Adonis, his Lucrece, his sugared sonnets among his friends.[11]

He asserts that he is the English Plautus in comedy and English Seneca in tragedy.

In 1603 King James VI of Scotland came to England to succeed Queen Elizabeth as King James I of England.

The Lord Chamberlaine's men came under royal patronage under the name of The King's Men. This elevation in status meant that now the men of the company were the recognized servants of the King. They would wear royal livery, appear frequently at Court and take part in royal pageants and processions. There are many records of his activities from now on. He bought 107 acres of land for farming in 1602 and again in the same year bought a cottage and a quarter acre of land.

It was about this time that the Mermaid Tavern became the regular haunt of poets. The poet's gatherings there have become legends. Keats writes:

> Souls of Poets dead and gone,
> What Elysium have ye known,
> Happy field or mossy cavern,
> Choicer than the Mermaid Tavern.[12]

Another epidemic struck London in 1603 and he returned to Stratford. It was at this time that the great tragedies got written. *Hamlet* was performed in 1602. It is the last of his plays written during the reign of Queen Elizabeth. *Othello* was performed at Court in 1604 and *King Lear* and *Macbeth* in 1606. The Problem Plays and the Chronicles were also being written at this time. The accession of King James to the throne brought about many changes in society as well as in Shakespeare's writings. This change is a very noticeable one. One of his biographers, F.E. Halliday, has pointed this out:

> ...a change not only of matter, but of manner as well, of the dramatic medium and vehicle of his theme, for the one demanded and necessitated the other, and it is possible to make a broad distinction between his Elizabethan and his Jacobean poetry.[13]

The plague year of 1603 saw the production of both the problem play *Measure for Measure* and the Golden comedy *As You Like It*. Both were performed at the end of the year at Wilton before the King. This place has become famous because it was here that *Arcadia* was written by Sir Philip Sidney.

Shakespeare was now spending his summers at home, thus dividing his time between London and Stratford. His first grandchild was born in 1608 and towards the end of the same year his mother passed away. His time in London too was drawing to a close for he would be staying there for only three more years. The time was ripe for his Last Romances.

The darkness of the problem comedies and the tragedies receded into the past, the pomp and circumstance of the history plays was left behind and a serene pastoral world was now revealing itself. The sonnets which had been circulating among his friend, were published in 1609 and in 1611 he retired to Stratford. *The Winter's Tale* was performed this year.

He still continued to come to London on some business or other till the very end of his life. For example he bought the Blackfriar Gate House in 1613. It is also thought that when *The Tempest* was staged in 1612 in order to celebrate a royal betrothal that Shakespeare took part in the performance. He acted in the role of Prospero and blessed the royal couple from the stage. In 1616 his will was drawn up and can still be seen in Somerset House. He passed away on April 23, his fifty-second birthday.

An elaborate tomb was constructed over his grave. There is a bust of the poet writing with a quill. Two corinthian columns at the two corners support a cornice. Shakespeare's coat-of-arms is displayed between these two, the entire thing surmounted by a skull. Under the bust of the poet there is a tablet with a Latin couplet and and English sextet inscribed on it. On the grave itself there is a quatrain which, it is thought, was written by the poet himself:

Good friend, for Jesus sake forbeare
To dig the dust enclosed here!
Blest be the man yt spares these stones,
And curst be he yt moves my bones.[14]

(B) SHAKESPEARE'S WORKS

A Chronological Table

The table given below has been drawn up by his biographers on the basis of the entries made in the Stationer's Register, Henslowe's Diary which recorded the dates of the performances of some of the plays and certain other such sources. Modern critics are more or less in agreement over the chart that follows. There is, however, a lot of overlapping.

Phase I

1591 — *The Comedy of Errors.*

'92 — *The Two Gentlemen of Verona, Henry VI, I, II, III.*

'93 — *King Richard III, Romeo and Juliet, Venus and Adonis.*

Phase II

'94 — *The Rape of Lucrece, The Sonnets, Titus Andronicus, King Richard II, A Midsummer Night's Dream, Love's Labour's Lost, King John, The Taming of the Shrew.*

'95 — *The Merchant of Venice.*

'97 — *Henry IV*, Pt *I.*

'98 — *Henry IV*, Pt *II, The Merry Wives of Windsor.*

'99 — *King Henry V, Much Ado About Nothing, Julius Ceaser.*

1600 — *As You Like It, Twelfth Night.*

Phase III

'02 — *Hamlet, Troilus and Cressida, All's Well That Ends Well.*

'04 — *Measure for Measure, Othello.*

'05 — *King Lear.*

'06 — *Macbeth.*

'07 — *Antony and Cleopatra.*

'08 — *Coriolanus, Timon of Athens, Pericles.*

Phase IV

'10 — *Cymbeline, The Winter's Tale, The Tempest.*

'11 — *Henry VIII.*

Different critics have divided his career into different phases. These are no sealed compartments. Often enough, they overlap, so the divisions become blurred and indistinct. There are, roughly, four phases.

The first phase is the phase of Experiment, lasting from 1591 to '94 or '95. At this time he was just learning his craft and mostly revising pre-existing plays. There is experimentation with rhyming and much use of word-play at this time. The art of characterization has not yet become worthy of notice.

The second phase is one of development. It stretches from 1594-95 to 1601. The Chronicle Plays and the Golden Comedies belong to this period. By this time he has attained mastery over blank verse and as far as characterization goes he is giving evidence of insight into the inner complexities of men and women. The plots become neater and better-managed.

The third phase is marked by the predominance of a sombre and gloomy mood. A keen awareness of the existence of evil has taken the place of exuberance and jollity. The Great Tragedies and the Problem Plays give evidence of this consciousness.

The last period, his Romance period, followed the third, the gloomy phase and lasted till the end. The four Romances were written at this time. These plays show Shakespeare in serene and majestic maturity. He has accepted evil as one of the continuing realities of life. Faith in repentance and youth shows a hopeful future for the human race.

It has to be mentioned here, as has been noted later also, that A.C. Bradley suggests that *Antony and Cleopatra* should be placed in Phase VI according to construction.

(C) NOTES ON INDIVIDUAL WORKS

The Comedy of Errors

This, according to many critics, is his first play. It was performed at Court in 1594 but that may not have been its first performance. The plot has been adapted from the *Menaechmi* of Plautus. It is a story of mistaken identity in which Plautus has one pair of twins. Shakespeare has introduced another pair, thus doubling the coincidences. The theme of marital relationship gains prominence in which the dramatist presents both the sides—that of the husband as well as of the wife, with equal sympathy, and this is not very common.

The Two Gentlemen of Verona

Many critics regard this play as the first of his romantic comedies. There are two pairs of lovers, two fathers and two servants. The characterization, thus, is very symmetrical. The theme is the conflict between friendship and love. The emphasis is on the first. Along with this there is the theme of forgiveness and reconciliation which appears here for the first time and will go on appearing till the very end, reaching its climax in the last Romances. Many of the features of his mature comedies are present here, like crossed love, disguised heroines, exile and flight. Julia is a precursor of Rosalind and Portia just as Silvia foreshadows Juliet. Lance the clown is the first of the clowns who appear again and again in his plays.

Henry VI, Parts 1, 2 and 3

Other dramatists also wrote history plays, but Shakespeare's are a class by themselves. If *Henry VIII* is included then he wrote ten of them in all. The pomp and pageantry of royalty is presented in captivating detail and serious issues like the duties of kings, their relationship with others, their human aspect, all are revealed in a fascinating manner. Over it all there is the aura of patriotism glorifying it.

The plays were based on the *Chronicles* of Raphael Holinshed, and were performed in 1592. This trilogy became so popular that it was staged three times in eight days. It ends with regicide, presenting scenes of ferocity and betrayal.

Richard III

The Henry VI trilogy shows the influence of Marlowe, and his play to an even greater extent. It is more of a tragedy than a history play. Many critics place this with the *Henry VI* plays and call it a tetralogy. The hero, King Richard III is a Marlovian figure but Marlowe's heroes are far simpler in comparison. This is the second longest play of Shakespeare (*Hamlet* is the longest) and highly stageworthy. The figure of Richard III dominates the play and since he meets with a tragic end the play gives the impression of being more of a tragedy than a history play. This is wherein it differs from the *Henry VI* plays.

Romeo and Juliet

A story of family feuds and star-crossed lovers, this play is centred round one of the most popular tales of the time. It is Fate that controls the lives of the two lovers and the kind of hero whose tragic error controls his destiny has not yet come into being. He has followed the original story very closely in this play. His talent manifests itself in passages of great lyrical beauty as the description of Queen Mab. He has also invented the character of Pertruchio, said to be a little autobiographical. The Balcony scene is one of the most famous scenes of all his plays and the characters have become classics.

Venus and Adonis

Ovid's *Metamorphoses* which he had read at school provides the story for this narrative poem. The poem was so phenomenally successful that it ran through ten or eleven editions in his own lifetime. The field of narrative poetry was new for him but he had many well-known narrative poems to guide him, specially Marlowe's *Hero and Leander*. It is a poem of great sensuous appeal and is composed in stanzas of six lines: a quatrain followed by a couplet. This pattern is a highly suitable one for narrative poetry and Shakespeare manages it with ease. It has been dedicated to the Earl of Southampton, who will later be known as Mr. W.H., "the onlie begetter" of the sonnets. There is no indication of deep passion in the dedication.

The Rape of Lucrece

This is the second of his narrative poems based on classical myths. It was dedicated to the Earl of Southampton and from the dedication it is clear that his friendship with the Earl has progressed far beyond what it was when he wrote *Venus and Adonis* (*vide* Shakespeare's life, *supra*). It explores the feeling of guilt and is thus a sombre poem. The stanza pattern used is the complicated Rhyme Royal, consisting of seven iambic pentametre lines, rhyming ab ab bcc. What raises the poem above the level of merely a well-written narrative poem is the psychological complexity with which Tarquin has been invested.

The Sonnets

Dedicated to Mr. W.H. supposed to be the Earl of Southampton, the sonnet-sequence is unique. There are a hundred and fifty-four sonnets, the first 126 of which are addressed to Mr. W.H. and the rest to the Dark Lady who is supposed to be one of the maids of honour at the court. This in itself makes the sequence unique for the other sequences by other poets are addressed to one person only. The last two sonnets, in the traditional manner, are addressed to Cupid.

The sonnets tell a story of intense love and no less intense hatred, for betrayal is also involved. How much of biographical truth is there in the whole sordid story is not known but the fact that he suffered intensely cannot be doubted:

> When my love swears she is made of truth
> I do believe her, though I know she lies,[15]

Titus Andronicus

This is a typical blood-and-thunder tragedy in the Senecan tradition that had immense popular appeal in his day. As has been mentioned above (*vide* his life, *supra*), it was a great success on the stage. It is a revenge tragedy that follows Kyd's *The Spanish Tragedy* in structure and theme, and contains a parody of one of Kyd's most famous passages. It is the first of his Roman plays, a genre that is going to be crowned by *Antony and Cleopatra*.

Richard II

This is the most topical of his history plays. The theme of the play is the problem posed by Ireland. Thus it reflects the contemporary situation to a very great extent. After seeing it the Queen exclaimed in anger: "I am Richard II, know ye that?... This tragedy is played forty times in open streets and houses." The play shows the deposition of King Richard II and this was such a sensitive issue that this highly emotional and important scene had to be omitted when it was performed. The character of Richard II is taken to be a study in weakness and is depicted with great sympathy and in passages of great lyrical beauty:

> For within the hollow crown
> That rounds the mortal temples of a king
> Keeps Death his court, and there the antic sits,
> Scoffing his state and grinning at his pomp.[16]

A Midsummer Night's Dream

This is the best of his early plays. It is thought to have been produced to celebrate the marriage of the Countess of Southampton, the mother of his patron. The beauty of the versification and the complexity of the plot give it a special position among Elizabethan plays. Fairy-tale characters have been given prominence. He is the creator of fairy-tale romance and he will use the mode in his last play, *The Tempest*. Three distinct levels of society have been presented here—the aristocratic society, the down to earth villagers and the fairies. Bottom the weaver is one of his most important early characters.

Love's Labour's Lost

This play is remarkable for its brilliant dialogues, particularly those of Lord Berowne and Lady Rosaline. There are four pairs of courtly lovers and quite a few humble characters as well. Lord Berowne, the wittiest of them, is supposed to be faintly auto-biographical, "a half-mocking and unconscious projection of himself". In a famous passage he decides to speak in simple language, denouncing wit:

> Taffeta phrases, silken terms precise
> Three-piled hyperboles, spruce affectations
> Figures pedantical: Those summer flies
> Have blown me full of maggot ostentation
> I do forswear them.[17]

King John

This play, though entirely historical, has yet a contemporary relevance. The topic of religion was a highly controversial one and Shakespeare usually does not deal with such topics, but in this play religion is not just an important issue, it is the central theme of the play. Just as Queen Elizabeth had carried on a life-long struggle with the Roman Catholic Church and had been excommunicated by the Pope, so had King John. Yet the play cannot be called a religious play. It is the relationship with foreign powers that is the main issue and the play is essentially a patriotic one.

The Taming of the Shrew

According to many critics this is the first of Shakespeare's plays in an Italian setting. It is a rollicking comedy, performed in 1594. There is confidence and maturity in the depiction of Kate, who is the Shrew of the title, as well as of Petruchio, who tames her. The main theme is the conflict between husband and wife as to who should gain supremacy in the family. This was a theme of great interest to his contemporaries. It was very successful on the stage as it gives hilarious entertainment. The theme of domestic relationship between husband and wife has been lightly touched upon here, but in the later plays it will be taken up far more seriously.

The Merchant of Venice

This is the first of the group of plays variously called the Happy or the Joyous or the Golden Comedies. The most important male character is, paradoxically enough, Shylock the Jew, who is the villain of the piece. His name stands for greed and extortion but he has been depicted with great sympathy. Portia the heroine is the most important female character. Very skilful use has been made of the convention of disguises as the three female characters all don disguises. An element of fantasy has been lent by the story of the three caskets. The play contains some of the most famous scenes of our poet.

Henry IV Parts 1 and 2

This play, in its two parts, marks the highest point reached by historical plays. Falstaff is, of course, the prime attraction of the plays—he is one of the greatest comic characters ever created. He easily overshadows all the characters, including Prince Hal. His rejection by King Henry V is one of the cruellest scenes in the whole of Shakespeare. Yet the rejection is justified for these plays are about kingship. Prince Hal could roister about with Falstaff and others but when he becomes the king the burden of responsibilities fall upon him and he has to leave that world and that life. The second part gains in psychological interest what it loses in comic entertainment. Falstaff however remains immortal. The serious issues are forgotten and "the fat knight" reigns in the memory.

The Merry Wives of Windsor

This is the only farce he wrote and that too on special order from the Queen who liked Falstaff so much that she wanted to see "the fat knight in love". It is thought that Shakespeare had poked fun at the humour characters of Ben Jonson in the person of Nym.

King Henry V

In this play the vision of the ideal king is given. Kingship and patriotism are the two themes of it. The poet presents both the sides of war—bravery and nobility on one hand and death and destruction on the other, with impartial kindness. King Henry is the ideal leader of men, inspiring his soldiers and leading them to victory. His victory is presented as well-deserved, for he pays for it, literally, with blood, sweat and tears.

Much Ado about Nothing

This is a double-plotted play dealing with the theme of love. It belongs to the group of Golden Comedies. The theme of physical love is there, and is portrayed as being based on external appearances. This is shown in the Hero-Claudio plot. The theme of the rejection of married love is shown in the Benedick-Beatrice plot. There is the love *versus* friendship theme too, but it has not received much importance. His craftsmanship is more mature, for the Benedick-Beatrice plot emerges as definitely being of more importance than the other, which is not the case with *Merchant of Venice.*

Julius Caesar

This is a political-cum-historical play. The main theme is the conflict between tyranny and liberty. This play was highly successful on the stage, particularly the Forum Scene. Every character is sharply individualized. This is the first of the Roman trilogy.

As You Like It

This is the most golden of the four golden comedies. The main events take place in the forest of Arden and so it is also known as a pastoral comedy. There are four pairs of lovers and at the end every Jack has his Jill. The main theme, as is expected in all romantic comedies, is love, and this has been shown on various levels, ranging from the courtly love of Rosalind-Orlando to the more earthly love of the shepherd. Disguises provide intrigue and in Rosalind he has given us one of his most captivating female characters.

Twelfth Night

This is the last of his romantic comedies. All the elements needed for a successful romantic comedy are present—disguises, mistaken identities, separation and union of siblings, etc. All these go hand in hand with superb poetry and characterization. There is a main plot with serious love-interest and a comic subplot. Sir Toby is a modified version of Falstaff. The play contains three of Shakespeare's best songs and one of his best clowns, Feste, who sings them.

Hamlet

This is the first of his great tragedies and the longest of all his plays. It is basically a revenge tragedy but the character of Hamlet is so overpowering that these other features of the play often get overlooked. Hamlet is apotheosized by modern critics as the typical intellectual, not just a tragic hero whose *hamartia* is indecision. Shakespeare has rarefied the blood and thunder tragedy of Kyd to such an extent that it has soared beyond the limitations of revenge tragedies.

Troilus and Cressida

This is the first of the problem plays in which the poet explores the seamy side of life. This is the closest he gets to satire, for the treatment of the subject of war and love is highly satirical. This play contains the famous speech on "degree" or social hierarchy which is delivered by Ulysses. Though the story is from myths the appeal is universal as well as modern.

All's Well that Ends Well

This too, like the foregoing play, is a problem play. There is some satire in it, but not as much as in *Troilus*. The basic theme is the conflict between virtue and nobility. This is given in the main plot of Bertram and Helena. There are several important sub-themes, for example the conflict between different generations. One of the instances that Shakespeare has stopped suffering fools gladly is to be found in the portrait of the braggart soldier in Parolles.

Measure for Measure

It is the third of the problem comedies, and has four marriages in it like *As You Like It* though the atmosphere could not be more different. It is the theme of justice that is prominent here, as it is in many of these later plays. The poet has used an old convention to illustrate this theme, that of the ruler of a place withdrawing and disguising himself to observe the true state of his kingdom.

Othello

Othello is the first of his works in the Jacobean era. It is the second of the great tragedies and has been called the *Romeo and Juliet* of the later Shakespeare. Like *Winter's Tale* it is a study in jealousy. Iago is one of the most remarkable villains of Shakespeare and Coleridge's phrase "Motiveless malignity" has become a famous description. The play contains some of the best poetry of Shakespeare which G. Wilson Knight calls "the Othello music".

King Lear

This according to modern critics, is his greatest play, for it shows man's place in the universe and has been called a cosmic Drama. Shakespeare took the story from several sources and adjusted the material to his own satisfaction and produced this unique play a sublime play. The character of the Fool in it has no parallel, for he is a very complex character, fulfilling many other functions besides the conventional one of a jester.

Macbeth

This is known as his darkest play—a tragedy of gloom and horror. It is usually thought that he wanted to pay a tribute to the king who was himself a Scot and so he chose a story from the history of Scotland. The play is specially notable for the character of Lady Macbeth who is often called the villain of the piece. Very effective use of the supernatural element has been made in the characters of the three Weird Sisters.

Coriolanus

This is the last of his tragedies. It is a political tragedy and a Roman tragedy. The hero is a born warrior and a patriot but his noble nature is in conflict with the sordidness of society. He is rejected by his country and joins his enemies, thus bringing ruin upon himself and his country. This play, along with *Julius Ceasar* and *Antony and Cleopatra* forms the group known as the Roman trilogy.

Timon of Athens

This play had never been staged and Una Ellis-Fermor has declared it to be an unfinished play. The hero is a highly satirical misanthrope and he withdraws from society. The play thus, does not end with the death of the hero and cannot be called a tragedy in the Elizabethan sense. It is divided into five Acts, yet the impression it leaves is of an unfinished quality in it.

Pericles, The Prince of Tyre

The phase of the last Romances begins with this play. In all these plays he is concerned with the theme of sin and repentance, which is followed by regeneration. This was a very popular play and shows how Pericles lost his queen and daughter at sea and after a long period of repentance got both of them back.

Cymbeline, The Winter's Tale

The theme of Separation, union and resurrection is repeated in these two plays as in *Pericles*. In Cymbeline the king loses his two sons and daughter and gets them back after many years. *The Winter's Tale* takes up the theme of jealousy as in *Othello*, only there is no death here. The king, after 16 years of repentance, gets his wife and daughter back. This play is always quoted as an example of flagrant violation of the unities of time and place.

The Tempest

In this last play Shakespeare has shown a most unusual respect for the Aristotelian unities. All the three rules of action, time and place have been scrupulously observed in it. It also covers a very wide range of characters, for there are superhuman characters in it (Ariel) as well as a subhuman one (Caliban). The theme of sin, repentance and regeneration is present as in the other romances. Prospero's great renunciation is supposed to represent Shakespeare's farewell to the stage.

Henry VIII

This is a history play, but Shakespeare is more concerned with exploring a theme than with presenting historical facts. This theme is that of patience in adversity. He had treated this theme earlier also (*As You Like It*) and here shows how the

King as well as the other characters learn patience. It ends on a hopeful note like the Romances, assuring the continuity of life.

The Two Noble Kinsmen

This is a dramatization of *The Knight's Tale* in Chaucer's *Canterbury Tales*. It is written in collaboration with Fletcher. Shakespeare wrote the major parts of Act I and parts of Acts III and IV. He did not collaborate with Fletcher any further as the latter brought in a rather sordid sub-plot, which Shakespeare did not like.

REFERENCES

1. Rowse, A.L., *William Shakespeare: A Biography*, London, Macmillan and Co. Ltd., 1963, p. 30.
2. Ribner, Irving, *William Shakespeare : Life, Times and Theatre*. Lond, John Wiley and Sons, Inc., 1969, p. 31.
3. *Ibid.*, pp. 38-39.
4. Quoted in Rowse, *op. cit.,* p. 58.
5. Halliday, F.E. *The Life of Shakespeare*, Lond, Gerald Duckworth and Co., Ltd., 1961, p. 60.
6. Quoted in Ribner, *op. cit.*, p. 45.
7. Quoted in Rowse, *op. cit.*, p. 100.
8. Quoted in Halliday, F.E. *op. cit.* pp. 102-03.
9. Rowse, A.L., *op. cit*, p. 201.
10. Halliday, *op. cit.*, p. 118.
11. *Ibid.,* p. 138. Also Ribner, I., *op. cit.*, p. 52.
12. *John Keats and P.B. Shelley: Complete Poetical Works* New York, The Modern Library, n.d., p. 191.
13. Halliday, F.E., *op. cit.,* p. 183.
14. Ribner, I., *op. cit.*, p. 64, as well as in many other works.
15. Booth, Stephen, ed., *Shakespeare's Sonnets*, New Haven and London, Yale Univ. Press, 1977, p. 119.
16. *The Illustrated Stratford Shakespeare*, London, Chancellor Press, 1982. *King Richard II, III*, ii, 160-63.
17. *Love's Labour's Lost*, V : ii : 406-10. This and all other quotations to be given subsequently are all from the edition referred to above, unless otherwise indicated.

3

The Story and the Genre

(A) A BRIEF SUMMARY

Antony and Cleopatra

Antony and Cleopatra (AC from now on) tells the story of a royal, or rather imperial love. It is one of the mature tragedies of our poet, for it is the last but one tragedy he wrote. In this play tragedy is caused, not by ambition as in *Macbeth* or by jealousy as in *Othello*. Here it is one of the noblest emotions in man, the emotion of love, that causes the tragedy.

It is necessary to know how Antony and Cleopatra came across each other. After the death of Julius Caesar his empire was divided into three parts and Egypt came to be Mark Antony's portion. At that time Cleopatra was the Queen of Egypt. When Antony came to Egypt he fell deeply in love with Cleopatra and this love was reciprocated. Their love for each other has become as celebrated as that of Romeo and Juliet.

Antony had, from the very beginning, been a pleasure-loving person and now, immersed in love, he began to neglect his other duties, that is, ruling the kingdom. This bred resentment in the heart of the other two of the triumvirs, Lepidus and Octavius Caesar. He himself was aware of his weakness and neglect well enough and when he comes to know about the death of his wife Fulvia and the possibility of civil war in Italy he decides to leave Egypt and go there:

> These strong Egyption fetters I must break or
> lose myself in dotage.[1]

He gets married to Octavia, Octavius Caesar's sister, on reaching Rome. Octavius is one of the triumvirs and it cannot be denied that the marriage is politically desirable, specially as Sextus Pompeius, called Pompey in short, is challenging the triumvirate at sea and on land. Octavius and Lepidus are preparing for battle and at such a time Antony's presence and co-operation is highly desirable. Both of them know about how Antony is luxuriously idling away his time with Cleopatra and despise him for it. But all the same they want him—Caesar makes it clear:

> A sister I bequeath you, whom no brother
> Did ever love so dearly : let her live
> To join our kindoms and our hearts.[2]

When Cleopatra comes to know of his marriage she is beside herself with anger and jealousy. She looks upon it only as a jealous woman, without paying attention to its political significance in any way.

The battle between Pompey and the Triumvirs however does not take place. Instead there is a meeting, a compromise is reached and a treaty signed. There is a banquet during which Menas tells Pompey that he can kill the three Triumvirs very easily to become "Lord of the whole world." Pompey refuses it with scorn as it would be dishonourable.

The treaty however is not honoured by Octavius Caesar. He declares war against Pompey and also insults Antony who decides to fight him at sea. In the famous battle of Actium Antony is defeated. This happens in Act III. The defeat is caused by Cleopatra. She had accompanied Antony and when the battle was at its height she fled the place, and Antony followed her:

> Like a doting mallard,
> Learning the fight in height, files after her.[3]

Antony tries to overcome his despair and shame at the defeat by making his love responsible:

> You did know
> How much you were my conqueror, and that
> My sword, made weak by my affection, would
> Obey't on all cause.[4]

Then the edifice of this love seems to be destroyed, for in Antony's absence Cleopatra tells Caesar's messenger that she is ready to surrender. This is a betrayal, not only politically, of Antony, but of love itself. Later when Antony (though he does not know about this formal proposal of surrender) accuses her of having ceased loving him, she protests loudly. Her attitude is not quite clear here.

The battle between the two armies duly takes place near Alexandria and at first Antony is victorious. But this fight was on land. Later there is a battle at sea. In this battle Cleopatra's ships again desert him and go over to Caesar. He realizes that he is betrayed and when Cleopatra asks for forgiveness berates her without mercy. Frightened by his violence, she withdraws into a tower and sends him the message that she has killed herself. Antony naturally believes the message and tries to kill himself in the approved Roman way by falling on his sword. But his attempt fails and though severely wounded, he does not die at once. While he is requesting his guards to kill him another messenger comes, telling him that she is not dead after all.

Hearing this, Antony, knowing that his hour has come, has himself carried to the monument where she is hiding. Seeing him carried thus, half-dead, Cleopatra's love for him flames up. The intensity and purity of Antony's love is evident as he does not utter a single word of reproach. Instead, with his last breath he tells her whom to trust among Caesar's men. Cleopatra's lament at his death are some of the best lines the play:

> O! wither'd is the garland of the war,
> The soldier's pole is fall'n : young boys and girls
> Are level now with men; the odds is gone
> And there is nothing left remarkable
> Beneath the visiting moon.[5]

It is very bewildering that even after this she sends a message to Octavius Caesar desiring to know what she should do. Not only this. When a deputation comes from him she tells Proculeius of her total surrender, only asking that Caesar will give Egypt to her son. It becomes clear that she had been waiting just to do this, for the minute she is assured of Caesar honouring her request she tries to commit suicide by stabbing herself. Her dagger is, however, taken away.

Frantic with grief for Antonio and mortified at her subjection to Octavius, she plans a different method for suicide and has a villager bring some asps to her in a basket. She puts on royal robes and crown and dies like a great empress and a great lover, with Antonio's name on her lips. Her attendants also commit suicide with her. It is left to Octavius Caesar to speak the epilogue:

> She shall be buried by her Antony
> No grave upon the earth shall clip in it
> A pair so famous.[6]

This is a very brief summary of the play, from which its beauty and majesty cannot even be guessed at. A far briefer summary has been given by Harley Granville-Barker:

> Antony breaks from Cleopatra to patch up an insincere peace with Caesar, since Pompey threaten's them both; he marries Octavia and deserts her to return to Cleopatra; war breaks out, Caesar defeats them and they kill themselves.[7]

(B) THE GENRE OF THE PLAY

There is not much scope for difference in critical opinions about the genre of the play, since it is historical in theme and tragic in outcome. This had been pointed out by A.C. Bradley who, though he does not discuss the play in his *Shakespearean Tragedy* (as he was to do later), yet classifies it along with a few others:

> *Richard III* and *Richard II*, *Julius Caesar*, *Antony and Celopatra* and *Coriolanus* are tragic histories or historical tragedies.[8]

Later he calls it a love-tragedy like *Romeo and Juliet*. Today it is generally accepted that it forms the third play of the Roman tragedy trilogy, the other two being *Julius Caesar* and *Coriolanus*. This play comes between the two in point of time. So even in this brief account it can be seen that there are already three ways of classifying it: historical tragedy, love tragedy and Roman tragedy. All three indeed are equally important. Later critics have added to the list. The most important of these is the one of historical tragedy so it will be considered first.

(i) Historical Tragedy

Almost all the critics agree in calling the play a historical tragedy, but many of them qualify the term by stressing the importance of love in it. As has been pointed out already, all three characteristics, history, love and the Roman quality are nearly equally important, each predominating in different parts of the play.

One of the first critics to draw attention to the historical element in it is A.W. Schlegel. He does not rest content with pointing out the historical relevance and realism of the characters and the events, but, what is far more important, considers the qualities peculiar to historical plays, underlining the difficulties of writing such a play from the point of view of the dramatist:

> In this consists the greatest difficulty of the historical drama:—it must be a crowded extract with a living development of history:—the difficulty however has, generally been successfully overcome by Shakespeare.[9]

As can be seen in the brief summary given above, the play is a "crowded extract", indeed, for there are many characters in it. There are thirty-two characters who have been named and three more with no names but speaking parts—the Soothsayer, the Messenger and the Clown. All of these are given in the *Dramatis Personae*. Besides these there are many more very minor characters who, though unnamed, speak a few lines in the play, like guards, soldiers, servants, etc. Apart from the speaking characters there are many more who provide a rich background to the play. The crowded quality becomes all the more evident as the costume of the Romans and the Egyptians differ remarkably, giving great variety.

The second difficulty pointed out by Schlegel is to give a "living development of history". This too is clear from the summary itself and will become clearer still from the scene-wise study in the next chapter. Many events take place in it, showing a continuous progress from the first scene to the last. History is created in front of the spectator's eyes. Antony goes to Rome and gets married to Octavia there, a peace treaty is signed, battles take place, feasts are held etc. It is true that the first half of the play progresses rather slowly, but "Living development" is taking place all the time.

There are likewise many flaws that a historical play is subject to. Schlegel has listed them, though he has not elaborated them or given examples. For example there are many events that are not actually shown on the stage but only referred to. The signing of the treaty between Pompey and the Triumvirs and the marriage of Antony and Octavia are two such events in the first part of the play. Agrippa proposes the marriage in Act I sc ii:

> By this marriage
> All little jealousies which now seem great
> And all great fears which now import their danger
> Would then be nothing.[10]
>
> Antony gladly agrees and so does Octavius
> A sister I bequeath you, which no brother
> Did ever love so dearly; let her live
> To join our kingdoms.[11]

After these allusions to the marriage Antony and Octavia are later shown in a scene in which she agrees to the marriage, but the marriage itself is not shown. The same is the case with the peace treaty. There are repeated references to it. Thus Pompey agrees to the terms:

> Thus we are agreed
> I crave our composition may be written
> And seal'd between us.[12]

There is talk of a feast to celebrate this signing of the treaty. The feast is shown, in quite some detail, but the signing itself is not shown. Such instances are to be found in the second part of the play too.

Another important defect of the play as a historical tragedy as pointed out by Schlegel is "Many persons of historical importance are merely introduced in passing." Three such persons can be mentioned here: Taurus, Lieutenant-General to Caesar, Canidius, Lieutenant-General to Antony, and Euphronius, the Ambassador from Antony to Caesar. These three characters have not been given enough importance in the play. The same could have been said about Ventidius, but then a full scene (III : i) is devoted almost entirely to him.

Schlegel points out a few more defects and then discusses the beauty of the play as a historical play. Here he stresses mainly the effective portrayal of the characters. The greatest critic of the nineteenth century, Coleridge, has no doubts about the play being a historical tragedy:

> Of all Shakespeare's historical plays *Antony and Cleopatra* is by far the most wonderful. There is not one in which he has followed history so minutely.[13]

Georg Brandes has united the play's historical qualities with those of domestic tragedy, laying stress upon the former characteristics. In fact he adds in two ways in ascribing to the play the qualities of a historical tragedy. First of all he says that it is not an ordinary history play, but deals with "world historic drama", that Shakespeare gives:

> ...an action embracing half of the then known world, which he wanted for the sake of the concluding effect.[14]

This is an expansion of the concept of historical tragedy which is eminently applicable to *AC*—more applicable to it than to any other play. Brandes, thus, has not only affirmed the play's claim to being a historical tragedy but has expanded its scope in a manner no other critic has.

Moreover, he has joined it to the concept of domestic tragedy, which again is enlarging the scope of the genre to which *AC* has been allocated:

> The greatness of the world-historical drama proceeds from the genius with which he has entwined the private relations of the two lovers with the course of history and the fate of empires.[15]

This is a very neat classification. Usually it is a problem for the *critics* to allocate it to any one genre—historical or romantic. Brandes has not quite side-tracked the problem but has offered a very neat solution to it which at the same time pinpoints the basic nature of the play. He does not call it a pure and simple domestic tragedy because it is not one, nor does he call it just a historical tragedy which would be too dry a name for it. No feature of Shakespeare's plays can even, be explained away by just one neat label. So he calls it a tragedy of world-history, interwoven with domestic tragedy.

A.C. Bradley however, gives two opinions on this subject. First of all he grants that it is a historical tragedy, grouping it with four other such as has already been quoted above. Then, a few pages later he classifies it as a love-tragedy which is a topic to be discussed later. Though he has not discussed the play in detail in his book *Shakespearean Tragedy* yet later he did discuss it individually. Taking both the books together, there are certain defects that he points out in the play as a historical tragedy. He has given seven general defects of Shakespearean tragedies in the book of that name, of which one is particularly applicable to *AC* as a historical tragedy:

> Shakespeare strings together a number of scenes, some very short, in which the dramatis personae are frequently changed...it appears most decidedly when the historical material was undramatic, as in the middle part of *AC*.[16]

This will become amply evident in the scene-wise analysis (*vide* Chapt. 4 *infra*) of the play. One after another short scenes succeed each other and many new characters are introduced. Looked at positively, this might be regarded as introducing variety and increasing the range, but Bradley considers this feature to be a defect.

There are two more defects he points out in the chapter devoted exclusively to *AC*. These are (1) a dearth of memorable scenes. He describes them:

> Scenes of action or passion which agitate the audience with alarm, horror, painful expectation or absorbing sympathy and antipathy.[17]

He cites a few examples to explain what he means, giving five such scenes from *Julius Caesar* and says that there is "almost nothing" resembling such scenes in the first three Acts of *AC*. It is in the second part of the play that a few such scenes are to be found. This detracts from its effectiveness.

(2) Shakespeare presents Antony and Cleopatra as beings so much superior to their circumstances that for both of them it is a world well lost for the sake of love. This is felt by the audience and the reader—a feeling that in losing sovereignty over this mundane, petty world they are not losing much. This lessens the tragic effect of the play. Pity and terror are not felt in such intensity as they should be:

> The greatness of Antony and Cleopatra in the their fall is so much heightened in contrast with the world they lost and the conqueror who wins it, that the positive element in the final tragic impression, the element of reconciliation, it strongly emphasized.[18]

This is a very serious flaw as it goes against the very spirit of tragedy. Any feature that lessens the tragic effect of a play is a very serious defect, but often such defects are lost sight of because they depend upon the grandeur with which the tragic protagonist is invested. The same problem occurs, in a much more intense form, at the end of Webster's *The Duchess of Malfi* and T.S. Eliot's *Murder in the Cathedral.* Both of the tragic characters in these two are invested with spiritual elevation so that the tragic effect is partially lost. The problem is not so acute in this play because both of the characters are perceptibly human, though heroic and grand. Even then one feels the hollowness of the world they leave behind them and thus to a certain extent the tragic catharsis of the play suffers. Eliot's play, indeed is not taken to be a tragedy.

Some years later the same point had been stressed by Una Ellis-Fermor. It is not that she classes the play as a love-tragedy, but that she affirms the positive quality of their love which influences the tragic effect of the play:

> In the final act there is so much less of pain than in *Timon*, *Lear* or *Hamlet* that we hardly think of it as

> tragedy. So little are glances of the actors cast back upon the lives they are leaving...that the world of actuality dims and dislimbs in the clear illumination of their faith.[19]

Critics have gone on considering the play as a historical tragedy but no important additions have been made in this respect by later critics.

(ii) Love-tragedy or Romantic Tragedy

Though everyone concedes the importance of the theme of love in the play, yet there are very few who classify it as a love-tragedy or romantic tragedy. The only modern critic who has done so is A.C. Bradley and there are a few earlier critics, of whom Coleridge is the most important:

> This play should be perused in mental contrast with *Romeo and Juliet* : as the love of passion and appetite opposed to the love of affection and instinct.[20]

Bradley has declared it to be a love-tragedy in an unequivocal manner and yet it is he who, as unequivocally, states that it is a historical tragedy and discusses it as such. As a historical tragedy he puts it within the group of other such plays, and as a love-tragedy he pairs it, like Coleridge, with *Romeo and Juliet.* While discussing the topic of the tragic protagonist he says that tragedies are primarily the story of one person, or at most of two, the hero and the heroine:

> Moreover, it is only in the love-tragedies, *Romeo and Juliet* and *Antony and Cleopatra* that the heroine is as much the centre of the action as the hero.[21]

He does not elaborate this point much, except to say that while the heroes of the early tragedy can be said to be of "intellectual nature and reflective habit" the later heroes are by nature passionate:

> The later heroes...Antony, Coriolanus have, one and all, passionate natures and, speaking roughly, we may attribute the tragic failure in each of these cases to passion.[22]

This indeed is very true as even a cursory glance at the play serves to prove. All Antony's weaknesses in this play proceed from this one cause: his love for Cleopatra. His failure in the battle against Caesar and more than anything else his suicide, is the result of his move. Bradley had mentioned *Romeo and Juliet* and *AC* together as love-tragedies and it has to be remembered that both Romeo and Antony commit suicide in the belief that their loved ones are dead.

This love, however, he is careful to point out, does not just cause Antony's downfall, but, on the other hand, ennobles and elevates him:

> [But] the passion that ruins Antony also exalts him, he touches the infinite in it.[23]

It is the same with Cleopatra. Her character, as also Antony's, will be analysed more in detail in the relevant Chapter (*vide* Ch. 6 *infra)*. Here the views of Bradley are the only necessary ones, and he, like almost everyone who comes into contact with her, is bewitched. He points out that Shakespeare has paid her the "unique complement" of devoting the entire last Act to her, in which she attains to tragic status. It is true that she betrays Antony again and again, yet it is as a glorious woman who gives up her life for her love that she lives in the memory of the audience as well as the reader. She has been criticised for her promisquity as she has been the mistress of Pompey and Julius Caesar before she met Antony, and has been called a "royal trull" and a "courtesan of generals" etc., yet it is as a lover that she gains tragic dignity in the play. Though the play is based on history yet it can be called a love-tragedy with as much justification as the term is applied to *Romeo and Juliet*.

(iii) Roman Tragedy

AC has been classified as a Roman tragedy by many critics. As a matter of fact Roman tragedy is a term that is included within historical tragedy except that the group of historical tragedy is much larger. There are only three plays within the group of Roman tragedies: *Julius Caesar*, *AC* and *Coriolanus*. These three have often been called the Roman trilogy, though that is not quite correct as the last named is not concerned with the story of Julius Caesar and Antony. Again, within the group of Roman tragedies two more plays can be included, *Titus Andronicus* and *Timon of Athens* but there are reasons for not including them. What is clear is that *AC* can not only be called a Roman tragedy but can be treated as a sequel to *Julius Caesar*. In spite of this fact it is a great tragedy on its own.

As early as 1680 Nahum Tate had remarked on its features as a Roman tragedy:

> He never touches on a Roman story but the persons, the passages, the manners, the circumstances, the ceremonies, all are Roman.[24]

He also points out with great perspicacity that Antony is not merely a Roman character, but much more. He is a highly individualized person who is, moreover, true to history:

> And what relishes yet of a much more exact knowledge, you do not only see a Roman in its hero, but the particular genius of the man, without the least mistake of his character, given him by their best historian.[25]

It is true that out of the thirty-eight scenes in the play only six take place in Rome but it must not be forgotten that the other scenes are located, if not in Rome itself, definitely within the Roman empire. As far as the characters go, 27 out of the 32 named characters are Roman and there are also persons like messengers, attendants, etc. It has to be also kept in mind that the other characters, though Egyptians, are still subjects of the Roman empire.

A.W. Sehlegel, as has been pointed out above, considers the play as a historical tragedy, but he emphasizes the Roman Characteristics, as it is quite unavoidable:

> The public life of ancient Rome is called up from its grave and exhibited before out eyes with the utmost grandeur and freedom of the dramatic form.[26]

There is one mo re reason for calling the play a Roman tragedy: the tragic fate that overtakes the hero and the heroine can be said to overtake Rome itself. It is true that the play takes place in the very beginning of the establishment of the Roman empire. Augustus was the first emperor and the empire was to expand and continue for centuries afterwards. What came to an end with the death of Antony was the Republic of Rome. That, no less than Antony, had a tragic end:

> Just as Antony's ruin results from his connection with Cleopatra, so does the fall of the Roman Republic.[27]

Keeping this in mind the play is indeed a Roman tragedy because with Antony's death the Triumvirate also came to an end, leaving Octavius the sole leader of the then known world. This took place fourteen years after Caesar's assassination and it is true that this implication of Antony's death is lost sight of in the evocation of pity and terror in the death of the hero and the heroine, but it is equally true a fact. This has not been pointed out in the play, it is left for posterity to infer.

The interweaving of Roman mode and the Egyptian goes on throughout the play and has been noticed by nearly everyone. Granville-Barker for example, considers the play to be a pattern of contrasts, and points out the contrast between the two lifestyles—Roman and Egyptian—as the very first of these,

> ...for a broad picturesque contrast Rome and Egypt are set against each other, and this opposition braces the whole body of the play.[28]

In this view the two themes run parallel to each other, sometimes one of them coming dominant and at times the other.

Granville-Barker finds both of these themes to be equally important, but in view of the arguments advanced by the critics to be given above, it has to be conceded that if one has to choose between calling the play a Roman tragedy or an Egyptian one, it is the former that will be chosen. Many (like Derek Traversi) have called it a Roman tragedy, but no one an Egyptian one. It is mainly because so many characters are Roman and moreover it signifies the fall of the Roman Republic that it has been called as such. Indeed *Julius Caesar* and *AC*, both can be treated as documents dealing with the foundation and the dissolution of the Roman Republic.

REFERENCES

1. Act I, sc. ii, ll. 118-19.
2. Act II, sc. ii, ll. 154-56.
3. III : viii : 27-28.
4. III : ix : 65-68.
5. IV : xiii : 65-69.
6. V: ii : 359-61.
7. Granville-Barker, H., *The Play's Construction* in Brown, John Russell ed., *Shakespeare : Antony and Cleopatra: A Case-Book*, London, Macmillan, 94, p. 87.
8. Bradley, A.C., *Shakespearean Tragedy*, London, Macmillan and Co. Ltd., 1960 rpt., p. xv.
9. Schlegel, A.W., in Brown, J.R. *op. cit.*, p. 27.
10. I: ii : 137-39.
11. I : ii : 156-58.
12. II : vi : 57-59.
13. Brown, J.R., *op. cit.*, p. 65.
14. Brandes, G., in Brown, J.R. *op. cit.*, p. 44.
15. *Ibid.*, p. 45.
16. Bradley, *op. cit.*, p. 55.
17. Bradley, A.C., *Shakespeare's Antony and Cleopatra* in Brown, J.R., *op. cit.*, p. 68.
18. *Ibid.*, p. 74.
19. Ellis-Fermor, *The Jacobean Drama*, London, Methuen, 1960, p. 267.
20. Coleridge, in Brown, J.R., *op. cit.*, p. 29.
21. Bradley, A.C., *op. cit.*, p. 2.
22. *Ibid.*, p. 64.
23. *Ibid.*
24. Nahum Tate in Brown, *op. cit.*, p. 26.
25. *Ibid.*
26. Schlegel, A.W., in *ibid.*, p. 27.
27. Brandes, Georg in *ibid.*, p. 45
28. Granville-Barker, *op. cit.*, p. 87.

4

A Scene-wise Analysis of the Play

ACT I, SC. I

This opening scene instantly sets the tone of the play. The dialogue between the two chorus characters, Demetrius and Philo, tells us how Antony has earned the scorn of his friends and followers by leading a life of blind love, with Cleopatra. Philo goes to the extent of saying, in a well-known sentence:

> The triple pillar of the world transform'd
> Into a strumpet's fool.[1]

This is said before the entrance of the hero and the heroine. As soon as they enter, the dialogue, which is at a very high pitch, lifts the play on to a higher plane, very much as Othello's speeches do in *Othello* (*vide* Chap. 10, *infra*.)

> *Cleo*.: If it be love indeed, tell me how much
>
> *Ant*.: There's beggary in the love that can be reckon'd.[2]

Antony is so enamoured that he neglects his kingly duties, refusing to see the messenger from Rome. He could not care less, as he says, in some of the well-known lines of the play:

> Let Rome in Tiber melt and the wide arch
> Of the rang'd empires fall. Here's my space.[3]

As there is no Prologue to this play this first scene has to be treated as such. This is the case with many Shakespearean and Elizabethan plays. Those that have no separate Prologues often incorporporate it within the first scene of the play. Usually the scenes in a play are interlinked with each other. As this is the first scene it has no former scene to be linked to.

It looks forward to the next scene in which Antony sees the messenger from Rome at Cleopatra's behest.

The scene can be divided into three parts: (a) the dialogue between Demetrius and Philo, (b) dialogue between Antony and Cleopatra and their exit, (c) the second dialogue between Demetrius and Philo. The second part is the most important, but the first sets the tone. Referring to this part of the scene, Una Ellis-Fermor regards it as "partial prologue" and declares that it determines the mood of the entire play:

> In *Antony and Cleopatra* the mood is set briefly in thirteen lines which also serve as a partial prologue.[4]

ACT I, SC. II

In this scene we find at first Cleopatra's attendants talking to the Soothsayer who tells Charmian that she will outlive her mistress and her future will not be so good as her past. He tells Iras the same. We shall meet the same Soothsayer after this also, in Act II, sc. iii, in Rome.

The Messenger gives Antony the news now that rebel forces are attacking the kingdom from the direction of the Middle East. After he has heard the news and decides to leave Egypt and join the battle another messenger comes to give him the news of the death of his wife Fulvia. She had been fomenting rebellion against him, so he welcomes the news and decides once more:

> I must from this enchanting queen break off
> Ten thousand harms, more than he ills I know
> My idleness doth hatch.[5]

No sooner said than done. He calls Enobarbus and gives him orders to prepare for departure. He tells Enobarbus that he is needed in Rome. Sextus Pompeius (the son of Pompey the Great) is challenging the Triumvirate and has already gained supremacy at sea. Though Enobarbus has been averse to the idea of his going, he agrees with Antony on hearing this.

The scene is written in a mixture of poetry and prose. This is a well-known feature of Elizabethan and Jacobean drama. Usually the noble characters speak in poetry and the humbler ones in prose. In this scene the entire conversation between the

Soothsayer and Cleopatra's attendants is in prose. Then we have poetry with the entrance of Cleopatra, then again in the third part of the scene when Enobarbus speaks. It is surprising that he speaks in prose here, for one of the most celebrated passages of Shakespearan poetry, the description of Cleopatra in Act II, sc. i, has been given to him. Yet here in his dialogue with Antony he speaks in prose.

This scene is linked to the foregoing as well as the following scene. The preceding scene had told us that a messenger had come, whom he sees in this scene. Here the decision to depart is taken, and in the following scene we shall see how he breaks the news to Cleopatra and her reaction to it.

The scene is divisible into three equal parts: (a) dialogue between Cleopatra's attendants and the Soothsayer, (b) dialogue between Antony and the two messengers, (c) dialogue with Enobarbus. It is a neatly constructed scene.

ACT I, SC. III

Here Antony tells Cleopatra of his impending departure. At first she is angry and will not listen to him. This is because she does not know as yet about Fulvia's death and Pompey's attack. She thinks he wants to leave her because he has grown tired of her. Then when Antony explains the situation to her and tells her of Fulvia's death, she understands the need for his departure and forgets her jealous rage. Their love is, as it were, renewed at the prospect of the coming separation. This scene is an entirely domestic one, dealing with the quarrel and the making up between a pair of lovers. This kind of repeatedly renewed affirmation of love is a typical feature of this play.

The scene also serves as an interim scene between Antony's decision to go to Rome on one hand and his final departure on the other. As such it is automatically related to the preceding scene, and though not to the next scene, to the fifth and the last scene of this Act. The figure of the Soothsayer is present in Act II, sc. iii, so it is linked to that scene as well. In that scene there is repeated reference to his absence.

ACT I, SC. IV

This scene is located in Rome. The two Triumvir's Octavius Caesar and Lepidus are seen discussing the present political situation. Both of them heartily despise Antony for his amorous withdrawal from political life. It is not that they despise him for being in love with Cleopatra. What they do not like is the fact that while the time is one for action, for heroism on the battlefield, Antony is not responding properly to the situation:

> but, to confound such time,
> That drums him from his sport, and speak as loud
> As his own state, and owns,—'tis to be chidden.[6]

While they are still talking about this a messenger comes and tells them of Pompey's victory on the sea. The two of them, while lamenting Antony's absence, quickly decide to go to battle. They will assemble the council immediately and take whatever decision is necessary. The scene ends on this note.

This is not a very important scene. But it shows a change of location and introduces new characters. It makes the political situation at Rome clear and thus highlights the need for Antony's presence there. It also serves to acquaint us with the Roman's attitude to Antony's luxurious life. It definitely takes the action forward a step by showing us how these two characters prepare to face Pompey's challenge. As such it is linked to scene ii in which the news of Pompey's attack had been brought to Antony.

ACT I, SC. V

This scene takes us back to Cleopatra's palace in Alexandria. Nothing important happens in this scene. It just shows Cleopatra pining for Antonio in his absence:

> O Charmian!
> Where thin'st thou he is now? Stands he or sits he? Sits he?
> Or does he walk? Or is he on his horse?
> O happy horse, to bear the weight of Antony![7]

Alexas comes bearing a loving message from him and a gift—a pearl. The scene ends here with her writing a letter to Antony.

The, scene can be neatly divided into two parts with Alexas's coming falling in the middle. It looks back to sc. iii in which Antony announces his coming departure to her. It is the last scene of Act I, so the later scenes to which it is linked come in Act II. Therein sc v we meet Cleopatra again after an interval of four scenes that take place in Rome, and around it.

This, the first Act of the play has introduced all the main characters and some minor ones also. It has established the supremacy of the passion of love in the lives of the two main characters and in the play as well. There is not much of action in this Act. As a matter of fact *AC* is not an action-packed play like *Macbeth*, though it is one of his longest. It begins at a slow tempo, which builds up as the play progresses.

ACT II, SC. I

The scene has now shifted to Messina and to Pompey's house. This is the first time that we see him. He is the son of Pompey the Great, who preceded Julius Caesar and was defeated by him. So his son looks upon Julius Caesar and his successors (the triumvirs) as usurpers and himself as the rightful monarch of the empire. He is a popular leader and has got victories in all the battles on sea. He is almost sure of winning the battle with the Triumvirate. He is quite contemptuous of Lepidus and Caesar but is respectful towards Antony as a warrior, though not as a man:

> his soldiership
> Is twice the other twain.[8]

He feels alarmed at the news that Antony is coming to Rome and is afraid that the three triumvirs will forget their individual petty enmities and join together to give him battle.

This scene is important only insofar as it introduces Pompey to the audience. Otherwise it can be regarded as a link-scene, serving as a link between Act I and Act II. It is rather longer than link-scenes usually are, but its function is the same. It is divisible into two nearly equal halves marked by the entry of Varnius. Pompey has been mentioned several times in the previous scenes so it is linked to them, specially to Act I, sc. iv, and also to the next scene in which Caesar and Antony talk about Pompey's supremacy on sea: "by sea/ He is an absolute master".

ACT II, SC. II

The scene shifts once more to Rome, to the house of Lepidus. Antony has arrived from Egypt. He is deep in talk with the other about the means to be adopted in the battle against Pompey. Both he and Caesar are eager to make up their differences in the interests of the battle. They speak amicably with each other. Then, seeing that the talk shows a tendency towards developing into a quarrel Agrippa proposes a marriage between Antony and Octavia, Caesar's sister. Antony agrees at once, realizing the political advantages of the liaison, as indeed does Caesar too. So they shake hands over the agreement and then quickly turn to planning strategies of the coming battle. Pompey is a formidable enemy:

Ant.: What's his strength by land?

Cae.: Great and increasing; but by sea
He is an absolute master.[9]

The marriage however has to be gone through before they can prepare to fight. So now they go to meet Octavia, to learn her opinion about it.

Now a few minor characters, Enobarbus among them, are on the stage. They just talk, nothing important happens. Yet it is one of the most famous scenes in Shakespeare, for it is here that the celebrated description of Cleopatra comes. This passage has been given to Enobarbus and it will be discussed more in detail later (*vide* Chap. 10 Style infra). It is quite long a passage, covering in all fifty lines. In order to avoid monotony Shakespeare introduces four interruptions by the hearers Agrippa, and Mecaenas:

For her own person
It beggar'd all description....
Age cannot wither her, nor custom stale
Her infinite variety. Other women cloy
The appetite they feed, but she makes hungry
Where most she satisfies.[10]

Nothing remains to be said after this—so wonderful a description it is. We realize that even if Antony marries

Octavia out of political reasons his heart will still remain with Cleopatra for ever and ever. The scene comes to an end with Agrippa inviting Enobarbus to stay with him.

This is one of the longest scenes in the play, comprising 250 lines. In fact it is the second longest scene in the play, the longest being the last scene. It can be divided into three unequal parts. The first is the shortest, comprising only 14 lines, consisting of a dialogue between Enobarbus and Lepidus. The second part is the longest, containing 160 lines, lasting from the entrance of Antony and the others to their exit. Then comes the section with the description of Cleopatra. From the point of view of the plot it is the second part that is important but from other points of view, specially that of poetic style, the third part overshadows it.

As such the scene is thoroughly integrated within the play, being linked with the preceding as well as the following scenes. As far as the theme of war goes it is firmly linked to the scene immediately preceding it as well as the others before it, specially to Act I, sc. iii in which Antony bids farewell to Cleopatra. It is no less firmly linked to the next in which Octavia gives her consent to the marriage.

ACT II, SC. III

In this scene Octavia gives her consent to her marriage with Antony. She speak so little (two lines only) that only her compliance is understood. Whether she does it out of consideration for the political advantages, or because she is attracted to Antony is not at all clear. Antony however, tries to be in her good graces, telling her that he is not really as bad a person as she might have heard. He also promises that he will behave himself from now on. But her reply to this has not been given.

This is an important, though expected, event but what follows is not any less important. After Octavia and Caesar have left a Soothsayer comes (*vide* Chap. 7, *infra*). This is the same Soothsayer who had been present in Act I, sc. ii. He has accompanied Antony from Egypt to Rome. He delivers a warning to Antony, telling him that in the coming battle

Caesar's fortune will be better than his and so he ought to avoid Caesar's company. He should go away to Egypt as soon as possible. There is great nobility in him, but not in Caesar. Antony's guardian angel is overshadowed by that of Caesar, so he must avoid him. Antony enjoins secrecy upon him and when he has gone he says that what the Soothsayer had said is perfectly true. Always luck favours Caesar and not him. He also incidentally makes it clear that the marriage is entirely politically motivated, his heart is not in it:

> And though I make this marriage for my peace,
> I'the east my pleasure lies.[11]

Though quite short the scene is not so insignificant as a link-scene, because two events happens in it: Octavia gives her consent and the Soothsayer warns him. The fact that the poet himself attaches some importance to the Soothsayer is made quite clear in the speeches given to him. His dialogue with Antony is far longer than Antony's dialogue with Octavia. In fact it is the first premonition we have of Antony's impending doom. We know, with foreknowledge, that though Antony will go away to Egypt as he decides after talking to the Soothsayer, he will meet with a tragic end (though not by Ceasar's hand).

ACT II, SC. IV

This is nothing more than a link-scene, consisting as it does, of only nine lines. Lepidus, Mecaenas and Agrippa meet in the street and decide to start for the battlefield. So nothing, even of minor importance, happens in it. It just serves as a link between the preceding scene and the following one. It, however, makes one thing clear—that Antony and Octavia have got married.

ACT II, SC. V

With this scene we are back at Alexandria once more. Cleopatra is missing Antony so much that she cannot enjoy anything. While she is trying to find amusement in something,—music or fishing or anything else, a messenger comes from Rome. He gives her the news that he is keeping well and she rewards him with gold. At the news that he is friends with Caesar too she is glad, but then comes the bad news, that he is married to Octavia. She loses all control over herself at this and starts abusing and striking the messenger and finally tries to stab him, at which he goes away. Then she has him brought back and questions him in a slightly calmer fashion. On hearing that he is truly married to Octavia she tells Alexas to go and find out what Octavia looks like in detail—her age, her height her nature, everything. Then, a little calmer, she withdraws into her own room.

This scene is important because of two reasons. First of all because it brings Cleopatra the news of Antony's marriage and secondly because it reveals unseen aspects of Cleopatra's character. We have seen her as a woman before this—a woman who is capable of loving intensely. Here we see her losing all dignity and self-control, going to the extent of hitting an inoffensive messenger. She even threatens to kill him. This conduct is most unfitting for even an ordinary woman, let alone an empress. Shakespeare shows her as being without any sense of decorum and without pity as well. Her language and the stage-directions both make this clear:

Cleo.: The most infectious pestilence upon thee!

Mess.: Good Madam, patience.

Cleo.: What say you?—(Strikes him again)
Hence, horrible villain! or I'll spurn thine eyes
Like balls before me; I'll unhair thy head.
(she hales him up and down).[12]

Shakespeare's female characters rarely behave in so very crude a manner. This is an uncommon, not to say unique scene in this respect (*vide* Chap. 7 i, *infra*). It continues for a few more lines like this. When he enters for the second time, however, she behaves in a more controlled manner.

This scene can be divided into three parts, the first of them lasting till the entrance of the messenger. The second part begins with his entrance and lasts till he goes out, and Cleopatra sends for him again. The third part begins when he comes in for the second time. It has links with the third scene of this Act in which Octavia agrees to marry Antonio. It has no other links in this act. Instead it is linked to the third scene in the next Act in which we see Cleopatra again. In this entire Act of seven scenes, this is the only one in which she appears, and that too in a most unflattering light.

ACT II, SC. VI

This scene is located near Mt. Misenum, at the place where Pompey's army is camped. Caesar, accompanied by Antony and Lepidus, has also arrived along with the army. They are meeting to discuss terms before engaging in warfare.

The Triumvirate is offering Pompey the kingdoms of Sicily and Sardinia in return for which he has to, first of all, withdraws his ships, and also to send a certain amount of wheat to Rome. Pompey agrees to these conditions and it is decided that a treaty will be drawn up to be signed by all of them. They are all in a very good mood, complimenting each other and patting each other's backs. They decide to feast each other as well. They all go aboard Pompey's galley, leaving Menas and Enobarbus on the stage.

The dialogue between the two of them is a revealing one. Both of them are veteran soldier's and courtiers, astute as well as worldly-wise. Menas did not know of Antony's marriage to Octavia. The minute he hears of the marriage he deduces its political importance at once. Enobarbus goes a step further by prophesying that this marriage will bring about strife between Caesar and Antony, for Antony will never be faithful to Octavia:

> *Men.:* I think, the policy of that purpose made more in the marriage than the love of the parties.
>
> *Eno.:* I think so too: but you shall find, the band that seems to tie their friendship together will be the very strangler of their amity.[13]

This is because, as he explains to Menas, Antony will go back to Cleopatra and this will hurt and mortify Octavius, because of the dishonour done to his sister. So a rift will occur between him and Antony which might well lead to warfare. Enobarbus is a good judge of human character and also a far-sighted person, because things are going to fall out exactly as he says. Ironically enough, it is the bond of marriage, supposed to bring Caesar and Antony closer together, that will bring about the conflict between them. Were Antony not married to Octavia, his affair with Cleopatra would not have mattered, just as it had not mattered in the past.

This scene, like Act I sc. ii, is in a mixture of prose and verse. As a matter of fact, we are reading prose in the play after a long interval, for all the scenes between this and Act I, sc. ii have been entirely in poetry. The dialogue between Menas and Enobarbus is entirely in prose, as the extract given above makes clear.

This is a significant scene, for in it the battle between the two armies is stopped before it begins and a peace treaty is going to be signed. It is divisible into two unequal parts, the first being much longer than the second. The conversation between the leaders makes up the first part and the dialogue between the two minor characters the second. Enobarbus's envisionment of the possible future trouble between Caesar and Antony forecasts the tragic end of the play, just as the Soothsayer's warning did. The scene is firmly linked to the former scene in which the Romans and Pompey had been preparing for battle, and looks forward to the next scene in which there is the banquet referred to in this.

ACT II, SC. VII

This is the scene in which the banquet talked about in the last scene takes place. By the time the Characters enter the stage they are already half-drunk, as is apparent from the conversation of the servants. The Romans ask Antony all kinds of questions about Egypt and he entertains them with highly coloured accounts of the Nile flood and crocodile and such things. Menas has great difficulty in prising Pompey away from the group, for he wants to talk to him in private. At last he manages to get him alone and gives him a very dishonourable advice—that if he can get rid of the three triumvirs then he would have the world for himself and himself only:

> These three world-shares, these competitors
> Are in the vessel: let me cut the cable;

> And, when we are put off, fall to their throats:
> All there is thine.[14]

Pompey's answer is typical of an honourable Roman and also typical of the commander of an army. He does not deny that it is very good advice, but he also says that he cannot follow it for he is the host and such an act will be a dishonourable betrayal. Instead of telling him about it, Menas should have done the work himself:

> Ah! this thou shouldst have done
> And not have spoke on't. In me 'tis villainy;
> In thee, 't had been good service.[15]

This shows his astuteness as a soldier. Menas however, feels injured and decides then and there to leave him and join the other party.

The banquet comes to an end with a song and a dance. A drinking song is sung, welcoming Bacchus, the god of wine. This is the first and the only song in the play. After this the characters disperse and the party comes to an end.

This scene, like the preceding one, is partly in verse and partly in prose. The servant's conversation is entirely in prose and that among the others is mainly in prose with occasional passages in verse thrown in. As has already been pointed out, the noble characters usually speak verse and the meaner ones in prose in these plays.

In this scene the noble characters too speak in prose at times, including Antony. This is because they are all half-drunk and do not speak very clearly and cogently. Caesar, for example, says: "strong Enobarbus/ Is weaker than the wine". The scene also contains the only song in the whole play (*vide* Chap. 10 Poetic Style, *infra*).

The scene does not lend itself to neat divisions but even then it can be said that there are in all, roughly three parts in it. The first part consists of the servants' conversation in prose. The second part is the main part of the scene, up till and including the song. The third is the parting of the revellers after the song.

The scene takes the action forward in that it establishes the peace agreed upon by the chief characters, though the treaty is not talked about here. Menas's counsel and later his defection are the two important points about the scene. It is related to the foregoing scene because it is the result of the compromise agreed upon in that scene and also because this banquet had been mentioned in that scene. We do not see Pompey again, but he will be referred to in Act III: sc. ii, Act III: sc. iv, Act III: sc. v and Act III: sc. vi. So the scene can be said to be tenuously related to these later scenes also. The peace treaty is not referred to again, but the banquet is, in Act III: sc. ii.

This is the last scene of Act II which has 7 scenes in all. By this time the action of the play has gone forward, though in a leisurely manner. The main events that have taken place in this Act are two: (a) the marriage between Octavia and Antony and (b) the signing of the peace treaty between the Triumvirate and Pompey. As will be seen, neither of these occurrences prove to be long-lasting, because Antony goes back to Cleopatra and Caesar, going back upon the treaty, attacks Pompey.

ACT III, SC. I

This is a short scene and the action occurring in it is quite unexpected. Shakespeare has not prepared us for this scene in what has gone before. It is located in Syria and shows a scene after a battle has been won by Ventidius for Antony. This character had appeared on the stage once before this (Act II, sc. iii) but then he had been called by Antony to be given some directions and had not spoken a word. Here he is the main, almost the only person, who talks.

He has won a victory over the Parthian army and the whole of Parthia now belongs to Antony. At present Antony is in Athens and Ventidius is going there to meet him and give him the good news.

As has been said before nothing in the foregoing scene prepares us for what happens here, nor is it referred to later on, though Ventidius appears again. It can be said that the scene is connected to the general theme of warfare that is prevalent in this Act.

It has to be noted that this scene sets the note for this Act. From this point onward's there is going to be a lot of action in the play. The first half of the play had been leisurely in tone. In contrast the second half speeds up and is full of action. A.C. Bradley had pointed this out:

> The second half of the drama is more exciting than the first.[16]

ACT III, SC. II

Once again the scene shifts to Rome, to Caesar's house. In the beginning of the scene Agrippa and Enobarbus are seen exchanging the news. Then the three triumvirs enter with Octavia. Antony and Octavia are going to leave Rome and so this is a farewell scene. Caesar and Octavia bid a tearful farewell to each other. This is the only thing that happens in this scene.

This farewell between Caesar and Antony is a friendly and dignified one, with Caesar asking Antony to be good and kind to Octavia and Antony reassuring him on this point.

The main part of the scene consists of this farewell. It is preceded by the first part which consists of only 20 lines of dialogue between Agrippa and Enobarbus. They remain on the stage while the farewell is going on and they comment on Caesar's command over himself and how Antony had wept at Julius Caesar's and Brutus's death. These comments however, are contained within the farewell scene and so it cannot be said that the scene has three parts. It has only two parts, the first of them being much shorter than the other.

It is linked to Act II, sc. iv in which Octavia gives her consent to the marriage, because here she is shown as Antony's wife and is leaving Rome with him. It is also related to the fourth scene of this Act, for in that scene we see her and Antony in Athens. So it prepares us for the future of this couple, specially because of the way in which Enobarbus had talked about the future life these two to Menas in Act II, sc. vi. He had said there that Antony would not rest content with Octavia as his wife, that the marriage was an entirely political one. This scene, thus, shows the audience the two of them setting out presumably to lead their own domestic life, making us wonder about what kind of a family life they are going to lead.

ACT III, SC. III

This scene, located in Cleopatra's palace in Alexandria is a most entertaining one. In it Cleopatra talks to the messenger who had been sent to inspect Octavia and report on her appearance, deportment, etc. in detail (*vide* Act II, sc. v *supra*).

The messenger is the same one who had figured in the earlier scene. Cleopatra had treated him very roughly at first but had then calmed down. It is to be seen in this scene that the messenger has learnt his lesson as to how to deliver the information he has got. Last time he had been not only ill-treated but threatened with torture and loss of life because he had just reported the truth about Antony's marriage. Now he will have to report on her appearance, etc. But he has learnt that Cleopatra does not want to hear the truth. So he tells her what she wants to hear, not the truth. He answers her questions one by one: Octavia is not tall like Cleopatra, she is low-voiced and clumsy in her movements. Cleopatra is very pleased with him. The interview goes on:

Cl. Guess at her years, I pr'ythee
Mess. Madam
She was a widow—
Cl. Widow?—Charmian, hark.
Mess. And I do think, she's thirty.
Cl. Bear'st thou her face in mind? is't long or round?
Mess. Round, even to faultiness.
Cl. For the most part, too, they are foolish that are so.
Her hair, what colour?
Mess. Brown, madam, and her forehead
As low as she could wish it.
Cl. There's gold for three
Thou must not take my former sharpness ill.
I will employ thee back again: I find thee
Most fit for business.[17]

So the messenger gets rewarded for telling lies that please. Cleopatra oven apologises to him at the end (1.35 above), praises him for his astuteness and promises him future employment: all that a messenger could wish for and more.

This scene consists mainly of this dialogue with but a few lines before and after it, which also deal with his conversation. So actually speaking this scene cannot be divided into different parts, nor is there any need for it, as it is a quite short one, being of 47 lines only. It is related to the foregoing scene dealing with the same theme, Act II, sc. v. Both of these scenes present Cleopatra in a rather unflattering light. It is noticeable that in this scene she believes whatever the messenger says, for that is what she wants to believe. This is not the attitude of an astute queen.

ACT III, SC. IV

This is a very short scene between Antony and Octavia. It presents the continuation of a conversation that seems to have been going on for some time. Antony is anger with Caesar and Octavia has been trying to pacify him. But Antony has cause enough for his anger. Caesar has gone back upon the peace treaty signed between them and Pompey, and moreover, has belittled him:

> he hath wag'd
> New wars 'gainst Pompey; made his will and read it
> To public ear:
> Spoke scantily of me.[18]

He has no objection to Octavia's going to meet her brother and trying to make peace between them. He, however, is not going to sit idle while she does that. He is going to organize his army for fighting Caesar. He is very indulgent to Octavia, allowing her to choose her retinue and the manner and date of her departure. Now she is going to Rome.

The scene is significant on two counts. First of all this is the first and the only time we see Antony and Octavia together and come to see Antony as an indulgent husband. Octavia speaks twice in the scene and never does she reproach him. Secondly it gives a premonition of war. It is a short scene, consisting of only 38 lines, and is in one unit. It is related to the next two scenes, for in them we are told more about the causes of and preparations for the war that will bring tragic doom upon the hero and the heroine. In this scene and the next we see Antony's point of view, and in the scene after that we are told of the provocation he has offered to Caesar. So this scene, while it harks back to Antony's marriage, also prepares us for the impending battle.

ACT III, SC. V

Enobarbus and Eros meet in this scene and, characteristically enough, exchange news. This is a technique frequently used in Elizabethan plays to impart news to the audience. We come to know here not only that Caesar and Lepidus have declared war upon Pompey, but also that Caesar has accused Lepidus of betrayal, denied him equal share in the battle and finally imprisoned him on very flimsy grounds. This means that there are two triumvirs now instead of three and lepidus's portion of the empire, in all fairness, should be distributed equally between Caesar and Antony which has not been done.

Antony does not approve of Caesar's action in engaging in battle with Pompey, in killing Pompey and also of his treatment of Lepidus. This is perfectly understandable. Caesar has acted most dishonourably on all three counts and Antony, being a highly honourable person, nothing is more abhorrent to him. Enobarbus gives Eros the information that the navy is ready for battle.

This is a very short (24 lines) scene and a functional one, as it gives necessary information about the battle. It is a link scene between sc. iv and sc. vi, telling us what had happened when Octavia is absent in Rome. It, like the foregoing scene, prepares the audience for the battle that is to come.

ACT III, SC. VI

The location shifts once more to Rome. Caesar, Agrippa and Mecaenas are in conference and just as in sc. iv. Antony had listed Caesar's offensive actions, so does Caesar list Antony's objectionable actions in this. Antony and Cleopatra had been "publicly enthroned" in Alexandria. Then, in front of the public, he had declared Cleopatra to be the absolute queen of not only Egypt, but of lower Syria, Cyprus and Lydia. The rest of the kingdom had been distributed between his sons. Moreover, he had accused Caesar of cheating him of his portion of the kingdom won from Pompey, of having deposed Lepidus and also of having misappropriated Lepidus's portion of the kingdom.

Caesar, for the present, has behaved with temperateness and wisdom. He has sent letters to Antony, telling him that Lepidus had abused his power, and has been deposed because of that. The letter also says that he is ready to give Antony his dues of the lands he has conquered, but in return he too wants part of the lands Antony has conquered, so that justice may be done.

They all know that Antony will never agree to do this and they also know that they themselves are not going to give him his dues, "Nor must not then be yielded to in this."

At this point the meeting comes to an end as Octavia enters. Caesar welcomes her with great love. But he is angry with her because she has come in an extremely ordinary, unceremonious manner, not in the style that a person of her status should have:

> But you are come
> A market-maid to Rome, and have prevented
> The ostentation of our love.[19]

Octavia tells him that she has come to him in this way because that is what she had wanted herself. Thinking to please him, she says that Antony had not objected to her coming to Rome to meet him. He however, understanding Antony's motive better than she does, at once says that he did so because he did not want her to be there. When she is innocently thinking that he is patiently waiting for her in Athens, he is in Cleopatra's arms:

> No, my most wronged sister; Cleopatra
> Hath nodded him to her. He hath given his empire
> Up to a where....

Welcome to Rome;
Nothing more dear to me. You are abus'd
Beyond the mark of thought.[20]

Octavia naturally believes him, the more so because Mecaenas too supports him. Caesar, to his credit, welcomes her with sincere brotherly love. This is the last we see of her. She does not appear after this.

This too, like nearly all the scenes of the play, is an informative and functional one. War between Caesar and Antony is finally decided. Octavia's arrival sets the seal upon it. Constructionwise the scene is divisible into two nearly equal parts, the first part a little shorter than the second. This first part lasts till the entrance of Octavia and the rest of the scene consisting of the dialogue with her, makes up part 2. It is firmly linked to the fourth scene of this Act in which Octavia decides to leave for Rome. It is also linked to the following scene in which the actual battle is fought.

ACT III, SC. VII

This scene takes place in Actium near the promontory. The scene opens with Cleopatra threatening Enobarbus. The reason is that he had been against her presence in Antony's camp at the battlefield. She has defied all advice and has come to Antony and is angry with Enobarbus.

Antony enters after this short dialogue. It is clear from his agitated sentences that his army has suffered reverses in the hands of Caesar's army. Cleopatra, instead of sympathizing with him, taunts him for being negligent and this infuses new strength and determination into him. He decides to fight by sea. This is clearly not a correct decision, as everyone tells him:

Your ships are not well mann'd;
Your mariners are muliters, reapers, people
Ingross'd by swift impress: in Caesar's fleet
Are those that oft have 'gainst Pompey fought.[21]

But Antony is obstinate. All he has to say against Enobarbus's counsel is "By sea, by sea". While they are still trying to persuade him a messenger comes and says that Caesar has already come and conquered Toryne. He has barely stopped speaking when a soldier comes and pleads with him not to fight by sea. At this, Antony, Cleopatra and Enobarbus leave and Canidius talks to the soldier some more. Caesar's supremacy becomes even more clear in this dialogue.

The scene is a very important one as it shows us that Caesar is winning the battle and Antony takes a disastrous decision that will, inevitably, lead to defeat, and tragic doom.

Placed against the perspective of the entire play, this scene comes in the middle of it. In all there are 38 scenes in the play in the edition being used for this book and this is the 19th scene. This and the next scene thus occur in the very middle of the play. The pace of the play had already been increased in the beginning of this Act and from this point onwards the speed increases most noticeably. Events follow thick and fast. Nearly all the scenes have to do with the battle and each is related to the preceding and the ensuring scenes. This scene can be divided into three clear-cut parts: (a) Cleopatra's dialogue with Enobarbus (b) Antony's entrance and exit, (c) Canidius's dialogue with the soldier. Everything in this scene points to the eventual defeat of Antony and thus prepares us for tragedy.

ACT III, SC. VIII

This highly eventful and important scene shows the defeat of Antony. First we see Caesar with his army, directing his captain Taurus to keep quiet, not to fight. Then Antony deploys his soldiers on the hillside from where they can see what is happening at sea. Next Enobarbus comes in and cries out in despair that Antony has been defeated at sea. Then Scarus comes and gives more detailed information. A point had come during the battle at sea when things hung in the balance—victory might have gone either way. At that crucial moment Cleopatra made the defeat inevitable by running away from the place with all her ships. What was worse, Antony also left the battle and followed her in his ships. His navy was left entirely depleted and leaderless. He tells, with great mortification, how Antony:

> ...Like a doting mallard
> Leaving the fight in height, flies after her
> I never saw an action of such shame.[22]

Canidius says quite openly that Antony has but shown them the way by fleeing himself. He says he will surrender himself to Caesar as six kings had done already. Enobarbus is the only one who still remains loyal to him, though not for long. Soon enough, he too is going to desert Antony.

The scene is thus a decisive one, showing us the defeat of Antony. It is quite a short one (44 lines) but an eventful one. Being so short and the subject of it being just one thing: Antony's defeat at Actium, there is no need to divide it into different sections. It should be mentioned here that according to Plutarch his soldiers had fought on for hours and later had waited for many days loyally for him to come back to them.

This too occurs in the middle of the play, being the 20th among 38 scenes. As has been pointed out already, this and the foregoing scene, being the 19th and the 20th scenes of the play, occupy the middle position. Both are important scenes, the former slowing us Antony taking the wrong decision and this one showing the result of that decision.

The two are thus, causally related or in other words, sc. vii is the cause and this one the effect. This scene, besides being related to the foregoing scene in this way, is itself also related in very much the same way to the ensuring scene. That is, it becomes the cause, of which the later scenes are the effect. The defeat suffered by Antony in this scene is going to lead to the tragic end of the heroine and the hero—the one who flees and the one who follows.

ACT III, SC. IX

This scene takes place in Alexandria. Antony is extremely dejected and ashamed of himself. He tells his attendants to leave him and go to Caesar, for he himself is not only defeated, but what is worse, dishonoured. Then Cleopatra comes in and she is feeling so guilty at having deserted him that she does not dare even to speak to him. When he speaks to her it is not to blame her but to blame himself:

> O whither hast thou led me, Egypt? See
> How I convey my shame out of thine eyes.[23]

Cleopatra feels intensely guilty and begs his pardon, saying she had not thought that he would follow her. It is expressive of the intensity of his love that he makes it clear that there is no question of asking for pardon and giving it:

> Fall not a tear, I say; one of them rates
> All that is won and lost. Give me a kiss:
> Even this repays me.[24]

The only thing that he can do now is to sue for peace with Caesar and that is what he decides to do, though it goes against the grain.

The scene thus shows Antony trying to reconcile himself to his defeat and it also shows the triumph of love over everything. It is for this reason that the tragedy has been regarded more as a tragedy of love than as a historical tragedy.

The scene is divisible into two parts, the first being much shorter than the second. It lasts till the entrance of Cleopatra and consists mainly of Antony's two speeches. The rest of the scene, from Cleopatra's entrance onwards, makes up the second part. The first part is highly negative in mood. The same theme, that of his defeat, is continued in the second half but this time a positive note is sounded: "all's for love and the world well lost", love is seen as a compensation for all losses and humiliations. It is integrally linked to the foregoing scene in which it becomes known that Antony is defeated, and the next scene in which Caesar receives the message Antony has sent.

ACT III, SC. X

This scene, in point of time, comes immediately after the preceding one. In that scene Antony says towards the end: "We sent our schoolmaster/ Is he come back?" and in this scene the schoolmaster Euphronius has reached Caesar's camp with Antony's message.

The message consists of two requests, one for himself and the other for Cleopatra. For himself he just requests to be allowed to remain in Egypt. If Caesar will not grant this, then he wants to be allowed to live like an ordinary person ("a private man") in Athens. It is a humble request.

Cleopatra's request is slightly more ambitious. She bows down to Caesar's rule and only requests that her heirs be made the kings of Egypt.

Caesar's reply to this is that he is not going to grant any of the requests made by Antony. He is ready to grant Cleopatra's request only if she drives Antony away from Egypt or has him killed. It is only after this is done that he will listen to her. It is noticeable that he does not say what he is going to do with Antony. He has said that he is not going to grant him what he wants. But what is going to happen to him is not mentioned at all. Perhaps this is because he has not yet had time to think about it. Antony would be a danger to him whether alive or dead.

This is a highly functional scene, though quite a short one (36 lines). The fates of both the hero and the heroine are decided in it. It is true that the issue is not clear yet, for Antony's fate still hangs in the balance, and the same is the case with Cleopatra, but Caesar's unforgiving attitude is quite clear.

It is a very short scene, but there are three clear-cut parts in it. The first part consists of a brief dialogue between Caesar and Dolabella, the second of the dialogue between Caesar and Euphronius and the third of the dialogue between Caesar and Thyreus, after Euphronius has left. Caesar sends Thyreus to persuade Cleopatra to desert Antony. It is firmly linked to the preceding scene in that the schoolmaster had been mentioned in that scene by Antony in connection with the message he had already sent to Caesar and here he is seen delivering the message. It is also related to the next scene as in that one Euphronius comes and delivers Caesar's message to both of them.

ACT III, SC. XI

In this scene Euphronius is shown as having come back with Caesar's message. In the beginning Cleopatra is shown to be in a rather bewildered state. She ask Enobarbus who is to be blamed for the defeat, she herself or Antony? Enobarbus unhesitatingly puts the blame on Antony, for the should not have followed Cleopatra when she fled from the battle. He was the commander of the entire army, so he should never have fled, leaving the men leaderless. It was that which brought about the defeat. It was a shameful action.

At this point Antony enters with Euphronius. He has already heard Caesar's answer. In his own answer he sends back a challenge single combat (or duel) to Caesar. He says that Caesar is far younger than him ("he wears the rose/ Of youth upon him") while he has grown old ("this grizzled head", "me declined"). All the same he is ready for single combat.

The most appropriate comment on this is supplied by Enobarbus. Antony has been quite foolish in challenging Caesar, for Caesar has already won the battle. He can easily take Antony prisoner or even kill him with the moral sanction, if not the approval, of military code. He does not even have to answer the challenge at all, much less accept it.

Then Thyreus comes. He has been sent by Caesar with a proposal for Cleopatra. The proposal is that she should leave Antony and put herself under his protection. At once, without any hesitation, she agrees to all that Caesar says. But while the dialogue is going on Enobarbus has gone and told Antony of this proposal. So Antony comes in a furious mood and sends Thyreus away to be whipped. Then he berates Cleopatra quite mercilessly, telling her how she had been Cneius Pompey's (the father of the Pompey in this play) mistress and then of Julius Caesar, and then his own. She had also had other men.

When Thyreus comes back after having been whipped Antony sends him back, telling him to tell Caesar that he is angry with him. After he has gone Cleopatra manages to pacify Antony by swearing eternal and faithful love to him and he takes the decision that though he has been defeated at sea his land army is still there and so he will fight Caesar on land. Meanwhile he is going to enjoy himself by throwing a party for all the captains of his army.

The scene ends with Enobarbus's decision that he will leave Antony, if not now, then very soon. He will find some reason for leaving him.

This scene is quite a long one (200 lines) with a lot of action in it. Several important things happen in it: (a) Antony sends a challenge of single combat to Caesar, (b) Thyreus comes with a proposal to Cleopatra, (c) she agrees to this proposal, (d) Antony decides to fight Caesar on land. It is thus an important scene. It is linked to the preceding scene in more than one way. First of all Euphronius comes with Caesar's answer as given to him in that scene and secondly Thyreus comes with Caesar's proposal as given to him right at the end of the preceding scene.

This is also the last scene of this Act. The entire Act has been a very eventful one. As has been pointed out earlier, the play picks up speed in the second half. This part can be called the *epitasis* of the play (*vide* Chap. 8 Plot, *infra*) in which most of the action takes place. The epitasis takes in the fourth Act and sometimes even part of the fifth Act, though that is a rare event. In this play the *epitasis* starts with this Act and continues into the next. It is highly eventful and while this scene presents Antony's defeat, it also looks forward to the future battle on land. His land army is stronger than his navy, as had been pointed out by his advisors earlier (Act III, sc. vii *supra*). So there is hope yet for Antony, though Enobarbus is quite sceptical about his success in the coming battle.

ACT IV, SC. I

The scene opens with Caesar reading the letter Antony has sent him. As is but only natural, Caesar does not take it seriously at all, knowing he is the victor. He just gives orders that his soldiers should be given a feast and then prepare for fight by land on the next day. The last words he speaks and which ends the scene are: "Poor Antony": This is indication enough of Antony's future. His scorn and pity are both quite understable. Antony's pretensions are quite laughable to him.

This short scene can be called a link scene, linking Act III and Act IV. It harks back to the last scene, for in that scene Antony talks about sending a challenge to Caesar and in this scene Caesar receives it. Again in that scene Antony had talked about fighting Caesar on land, and in this one Caesar talks about the same thing. This battle is talked about in the next five scenes and finally takes place in sc. vii and sc. viii. So while this scene looks back at the preceding scene it also prepares us for the future. As a link scene, so, it is a very good one. It takes the action forward also by showing Caesar preparing for war.

ACT IV, SC. II

This is a very moving scene as Antony bids farewell to his attendants in it. His friends like Enobarbus and the other courtly attendants are there and he shakes hands with each of them. He shakes by hand all the servants as well and thanks them. His words make all of them weep and he finally dispels all gloom by telling them that he hopes for victory in this battle.

It is a short scene, not divisible into separate parts. Nor does it take the action forward, for Antony's preparations for this war have already been mentioned earlier. It can be said that it introduces the element of *pathos* which should be present in every tragedy, but otherwise it is not an important scene. This and the next few scenes are all inter-related as all deal with the coming battle on land.

ACT IV, SC. III

This scene present four soldiers on guard duty outside the palace on the eve of battle. It is remarkable insofar as it presents, for the first and the only time in the play, the element of the supernatural in an open, perceptible manner.

It is while the guards are talking about the next day's battle that they hear an unearthly music. The stage directions say "Music of haulboys under the stage." The soldiers are, as is but natural, very surprised and at first cannot make out where it is coming from or what it means:

1 *sold.* Music i' the air.

3 *sold.* Under the earth.

4 *sold.* It signs well, does it not?

5 *sold.* No.

1 *sold.* Peace, I say!
What should this mean?
2 *sold.* 'Tis the god Hercules, whom Antony lov'd
Now leaves him.[25]

This explanation offered by the second soldier is the one accepted by all, so perhaps this is what it means. Except for the fact that it is linked to the coming battle, this scene has no other relevance to the play. There is no reference to this supernatural music later on in this play; it occurs just this once. But it serves to heighten tension and apprehension in the play. Shakespeare uses many strategies to create dramatic tension and this is one of them. Here there is no ghost as in *Julius Caesar*, but this too is quite effective.

ACT IV, SC. IV

The scene shows Antony preparing himself for war. He is putting on his armour. Cleopatra also comes in to help him in doing so. While he is arming himself a soldier comes to tell him that they are ready. Then Captains and more soldiers come to take him to the field of battle. He goes out with them, like a heroic soldier, with hope and courage in his heart. This scene like the two preceding ones, is but a preparation for the war. As such it looks back to the former scenes and forward to the next. It carries the action forward, unlike the third scene.

ACT IV, SC. V

In this scene Antony gets the alarming and also heart-rendering news that Enobarbus has left him and gone over to Caesar. The dramatist had prepared the audience for this defection in the lst scene of Act III but Antony had had no inkling of it. It is in the battlefield that he gets the news, so there is not much time for him to express his shock and grief. It is typical of the nobility of his nature that he does not blame Enobarbus for this betrayal but rather himself. His nature and conduct is truly noble, for he directs Eros to send Enobarbus the treasure that is due to him and moreover, write a letter of "gentle adieus and greetings." He blames himself for Enobarbus's desertion:

O! My fortunes have
Corrupted honest men.—Despatch.—Enobarbus![26]

This is a very short scene, having only 17 lines, but it is linked to the last scene of Act III and to the next scene in which Enobarbus is shown regretting his disloyalty when it is too late.

ACT IV, SC. VI

This scene is located in Caesar's camp. He is seen issuing the order that Antony must be taken prisoner alive. When he has left with his retinue Enobarbus speaks. He is already regretting the fact that he has deserted Antony. While he is still regretting it a soldier comes and tells him that Antony has sent his treasures to him. He is full of self-blame and bitterness and is deeply ashamed. He cannot bear the thought that Antony has sent his treasures to him in spite of his disloyalty. He feels death would be preferable to fighting Antony.

This scene is related to the foregoing scene and the ensuing ones. Enobarbus's regret adds to the main human interest and it is related to sc. ix in which he dies of a broken heart.

ACT IV, SC. VII

This is another battle-scene and Antony's victory is proclaimed in it. Caesar had not expected such strong opposition and has now retired into his camp. Antony is left victorious. There are two brief dialogues with Scarus and Eros in which Antony's victory is announced. All of these brief battle-scenes are interrelated.

ACT IV, SC. VIII

This scene, located under the walls of Alexandria, shows Antony preparing to celebrate his victory. He thanks the captains and tells them to take rest and enjoy themselves. While he is still talking to them Cleopatra enters, greatly relieved and immeasurably happy. Antony introduces Scarus to her and she promises him an armour of gold. The two of them are going to make a triumphal march through Alexandria and Antony invites all those who are with him to join the banquet.

ACT IV, SC. IX

This scene is remarkable only in that Enobarbus dies in it. It takes place at Caesar's camp.

It is night and some soldiers are on sentinel duty. They see Enobarbus entering the stage. His grief and shame at having left Antony is so strong that it leads him to his death. Though there is nothing to indicate that he commits suicide, still he dies. He just lies down and dies and the soldiers carry his body to Caesar. It is a short scene (33 lines) and his death is the only event that occurs in it. As such it is related to sc. vi in which he had started to regret his defection and wished to die. It is not referred to again later.

ACT IV, SC. X

This, like the short scene before this, is an eventful battle scene. First we see Antony with his soldiers and come to know that this day's battle is to be at sea. Then Caesar enters with his army and says it will be better for them to fight by land. Then Antony and Scarus come and from the latter we come to know that Antony's navy is very weak and even while he is talking it becomes known that Antony has lost the sea-battle. He cries out in despair and anger:

> All is lost!
> This foul Egyptian hath betrayed me:
> My fleet hath yielded to the foe.[27]

It is the same story as in Act III sc. viii. Cleopatra has again betrayed him. Her ships had already been in a bad shape and now they have surrendered to Caesar, which they would not have done if not so directed by her. He is furious with her and when she comes in upbraids her in extremely strong language. Now he knows there is no hope for him and he decides to kill her.

This is a long scene in comparison with the ones that have preceded it. Moreover it is a very eventful one and can be divided into three parts. The first part consists of the coming in and going out of the two leaders, lasting till Scarus's brief soliloquy. The second part begins with Antony's crying out "All is lost" and lasts till the entrance of Cleopatra. The rest of the scene consists of Antony's driving her away and deciding to kill her. As is to be expected the scene is related to the preceding and the ensuing scenes. But it does not prepare us for the future. We are led to expect that Antony will kill or at least try to kill, Cleopatra. What actually happens is completely unexpected.

ACT IV, SC. XI

This is a very short scene of only ten and half lines. Cleopatra is very frightened. Charmian advises her to retire into the monument and send information to Antony that she has committed suicide. Cleopatra at once decides to do so and goes inside the monument. Thus in one stroke she has not only saved her own skin but completely disabled Antony as well. Only, she does not realize the serious, fatal consequences her message to Antony is going to have.

This can be considered to be a link scene with a difference. Usually such scenes are not of much importance—they serve only as a transit from one scene to another. This one is not of that kind; it is a very important scene, for, more than any other scene, this is the one which is going to lead to the ultimate tragic doom.

ACT IV, SC. XII

Antony is in a mood of despair. He has reached the point of no return. This is the scene containing the famous speech "Sometimes we see a cloud that's dragonish." The end of this speech, addressed to Eros, makes it quite clear that he is determined to kill Cleopatra first and then himself:

> Nay, weep not, gentle Eros, there is left us
> Ourselves to end ourselves.[28]

Then Mardian enters and tells Antony that Cleopatra has killed herself and that she died with his name on her lips. At once it is as if all the strength has gone out of Antony. The speech lamenting her death is one of the most moving passages in Shakespeare, comparable with the last speeches of Romeo, Othello, Macbeth and others such. He requests Eros to kill him. But Eros, instead of doing so, kills himself. Then, seeing no way out of it, Antony falls on his own sword to kill himself. It must be remembered here that this was no sin, as was later to be declared by the principles of Christian theology, and according to the Romans it was a highly honourable act, next to die fighting in the field of battle.

To Antony's misfortune, however, he does not die then and there. So he calls in his guards and begs them to kill him, as he has already half killed himself. But then Diomedes comes in and tells him that Cleopatra has not committed suicide after all. But the news has come too late to save him. Nothing can save him now and he asks his guards to carry him to the place where Cleopatra is hiding, so that he may bid her a last farewell.

With this scene the catastrophe or the denouement has begun. It is quite a long scene and can be divided into three parts. The first part lasts till the entrance of Mardian with the false news of Cleopatra's death. The second part is far longer and ends with Eros's death. The third part contains Antony's attempted suicide and his being borne off to Cleopatra's monument.

This scene is one of the most important scenes, hastening the play to its tragic end. It is related to the foregoing scene in which Cleopatra sends the false news and the next scene in which Antony dies.

ACT IV, SC. XIII

This is the famous death scene of Antony. It begins at a high pitch and the poetry soars higher and higher as the scene progresses. When the half-dead Antony is borne up to Cleopatra's window she cries out:

> O Sun
> Burn the great sphere thou mov'st in!—darkling stand
> The varying shores o' the world.[29]

Antony is brought inside so that a last kiss can be exchanged. He dies, making it clear that he dies an honourable death:

> do now not basely die,
> Not cowardly put off my helmet to

My countryman, a Roman by a Roman
Valiantly vanquish'd.[30]

Cleopatra's lament is one of the most famous passages in Shakespeare

The crown o' the earth doth melt.—My Lord!—
O! wither'd is the garland of the war,
The soldier's pole is fall'n: young boys and girls
Are level now with men; the odds is gone,
And there is nothing left remarkable
Beneath the visiting moon.[31]

Her later speech that comes three lines after this is not so elevated in style, but far more moving. She tries to cheer her women up. The strength of her character comes out superbly here. She says he must be buried in the noble Roman fashion. The scene ends with a Senecan couplet:

Come : We have no friend
But resolution, and the briefest end.[32]

This is the last scene of this Act and, as can be seen the catastrophe has begun with it, though some critics tend to put it a bit forward and hold sc. x to be the beginning of the catastrophe. There is no need to divide the scene into different parts, though on the stage Antony's entrance might be considered to be the beginning of the second part. It is better to consider the scene as one individual whole, for that will heighten the tragic effect. This is the longest Act of the play, containing as it does 13 scenes in all.

ACT V, SC. I

This scene is located in Caesar's camp. Dercetas has brought the new of Antony's death. He has brought the blood-stained sword of Antony as proof. Everyone is awestruck. They have only praise for him. While they are still lamenting his death a messenger comes from Cleopatra who desires to know what Caesar wants. Caesar reassures him that he will treat her honourably and then sends Proculeius to take the same reassurance to her. At the same time he tells him to comfort her in such terms as will prevent her from killing herself. He needs her alive to make his triumph complete. She must not cheat him by killing herself.

This is not a very long scene, and the main event it contains is the delivering of the news of Antony's death. It can be divided into two parts, the first of them dealing with Antony's death and the second with the entrance of Cleopatra's messenger. It refers back to the last scene in Act IV in which Antony died and looks forward to the next, the concluding scene. There is very little premonition of Cleopatra's death in it, but Caesar does refer to the possibility of her committing suicide when he instructs Proculeius.

ACT V, SC. II

This is the last and the longest scene (364 lines) of the play, continuing the catastrophe and containing the epilogue. It takes place in the monument into which Cleopatra had retired and where Antony died. After a speech of a few lines by Cleopatra, Proculeius enters, the messenger of Caesar.

On learning his name Cleopatra remembers that this is the man whom Antony had told her, with his last breath, to trust (iv : xiii : 48). All the same, as they enter the monument she realizes that she is a prisoner, no longer the mighty Queen of Egypt. She tries to kill herself with a dagger. Proculeius seizes it and tries to comfort her. Then Dolabella comes and he goes away. There follow some of the best passages in Shakespeare when Cleopatra praises Antony to Dolabella. She is nearly frantic with grief. Her outpouring of this grief is known as Cleopatra's ecstasy. It continues for quite some time.

Then Caesar enters. He speaks to her most gently and with great honour. She has prepared a list of her possessions and gives it to Caesar, but it is not an exhaustive list as Seleucus, her treasurer, tells Caesar. He, however, is not perturbed and reassures Cleopatra repeatedly of honourable treatment, telling her that he will treat her exactly the way she herself would like. She however does not believe him. She whispers something to Charmian and this, as will be clear later, is to direct her to have some poisonous vipers to be brought to her.

A few speeches later, in which Dolabella comes and tells her that she and her children will be exhibited in Caesar's triumphal progress through Syria to Rome, a villager comes with some figs for her. Actually he has brought her the snakes she had told Charmian to get, covered with figs. This villager has been called a Clown and his speeches afford comic relief for a few brief minutes. The dialogue with him is in prose.

Then she dresses herself in full regalia, with royal robes and crown. The speech that accompanies it is one of the most famous passages in Shakespeare:

> Give me my robe, put on my crown, I have
> Immortal longings in me; now no more
> The juice of grape shall moist this lip.[33]

Iras falls and dies even before Cleopatra has taken up the asp. After Cleopatra is dead Charmian also takes the asp and dies. When Dolabella and Caesar come it is to be confronted by the corpses. It is left for Caesar to deliver the epilogue in which he says that both of them shall be buried side by side:

> She shall be buried by her Antony:
> No grave upon the earth shall clip in it
> A pair so famous.[34]

This, the last scene of the play is the longest scene in it. It contains the last part of the Catastrophe and includes the epilogue on it. It is a very long scene and can be divided into several parts. These divisions have been given in different ways by different critics.

A tentative division will go as follows: the first part lasts till her attempt at suicide which is stopped by Proculeius. The second part continues from there till the entrance of the Clown. The third part starts with the entrance of the Clown and lasts till his exit. The fourth part begins after his exit and continues till the death of Charmian. The fifth part starts after her death and continues till the end, taking in the epilogue as well. These divisions however are arbitrary ones and fluid.

There are certain other points to be noted about this scene. One of them is that it contains prose dialogue, which makes up the comic relief afforded by the Clown. There had been two scenes with prose dialogue in them, Act I, sc. ii and Act II, sc. vii. In between lie the whole of Acts III and IV and the major part of Act V.

Another point about the style of this scene is that it contains a few of the best passages in Shakespeare. There have, been many fine passages before this also, e.g. Enobarbus's description of Cleopatra, but no other scene has so many passages in which tragic intensity mingles with intense love and pathos as this one. All in all this is one of the most effective scenes among Shakespeare's tragedies.

The tragic effect of this scene is equal to that in the scene of Antony's death. The intensity of tragic effect in this play, as has been pointed out in Chapter 3 above, has been called into question by different critics. This topic, as it has already been discussed, will not be repeated here.

REFERENCES

1. Act I, sc. i, lines 12-13.
2. I : i : 14-15.
3. I : i : 33-34.
4. Ellis - Fermor, *u*, *op. cit.*, p. 34.
5. I : ii : 130-32.
6. I : iv : 28-30.
7. I : v : 18-21.
8. II : i : 34-35.
9. II : ii : 166-68.
10. II : ii : 202-44.
11. II : iii : 40-41.
12. II : v : 61-64.
13. II : vi : 118-22.
14. II : vii : 73-76.
15. II : vii : 76-78.
16. Bradley, *op. cit.*, p. 42.
17. III : iii : 27-37.
18. III : iv : 3-6.
19. III : vi : 51-53.
20. III : vi : 66-88.
21. III : vii : 34-37.
22. III : viii : 27-29.
23. III : ix : 51-52.

24. III : ix : 69-71.
25. IV : iii : 12-15.
26. IV : v : 16-17
27. IV : x : 23-25.
28. IV : xii : 21-22.
29. IV : xiii : 10-12.
30. IV : xiii : 55-58.
31. IV : xiii : 64-69.
32. IV : xiii : 91-92.
33. V : ii : 279-81.
34. V : ii : 359-61.

5

The Major Themes

Not every play can gain the status of a great universal work of art. In addition to many other requirements, it has to have a theme that holds it together, giving it coherence and unity. The plot might scrupulously adhere to all the classical rules, yet the absence of a unifying theme will give an impression of chaos. It is always desirable that the dramatist have an idea to expound—an idea that may be a religious or philosophical idea, or a moral message or an aesthetic idea. The whole process differs from writer to writer. Sometimes he may have such an idea or theme, in his mind from the very beginning and sometimes it may develop as he writes. It may often happen, as is the case with our poet, that the ideas in the mind of the dramatist may not be known to the reader and it will be after a close study that the unifying theme is found. The difficulty in such a case is that the interpretation will differ with each individual reader, which is what has happened with our poet. His mature plays have given rise to many interpretations and even *AC*, a historical play, has given rise to quite a few of them. The variety in critical opinion however, should not be taken to signify vagueness. It is the other way round. The multiplicity of meanings signify the rich complexity of the work. Another feature is there that adds to this complexity. There might be more than one theme to a play. There might be a central theme enriched by many subsidiary ones. Henri Fluchère has said:

> There are minor themes, ceremonial themes, major themes, symbolic themes; sometimes set out *en clair*,

> sometimes developed at length and sometimes, on the contrary, just suggested.[1]

When discussing the themes in any play of Shakespeare, all these factors will have to be kept in mind. *AC*, being a historical play, might seem to be simple, but it will be seen that there is room for variety even here.

(A) THE THEME OF LOVE

There can never be any doubt as to the fact that this is the overriding theme of the play. Antony and Cleopatra have been accepted, like Romeo and Juliet, as the prototype of lovers who sacrificed their life and the world itself for love. Indeed, Dryden's play is named *All for Love: or The World Well Lost.* There are betrayals on the part of Cleopatra, but Antony's love never swerves. It is true that he marries Octavia, but it is made quite clear at the time that it is for political reasons, not because he has fallen in love with her. As a matter of fact he goes back to Cleopatra as soon as possible, follows her when she leaves him during the sea-battle because of which he is defeated in that battle, and at the end, as soon as he hears that she is dead, tries to kill himself and does finally kill himself. He gets proof of her perfidy again and again in the play and upbraids her again and again—the most strongly in Act IV, sc. x. But as soon as he hears of her death life becomes meaningless for him:

> I'll o'ertake thee, Cleopatra, and
> Weep for my pardon. So it must be, for now
> All length is torture; since the torch is out,
> Lie down and stray no further.[2]

The same is the case with Cleopatra. She had been the mistress of Pompey and of Julius Caesar before she had met him, and she betrays him repeatedly in the course of the play. Yet when he is gone the world becomes hollow and meaningless for her:

> Shall I abide
> In this dull world which in thy absence is
> No better than a sty?[3]

There is never any doubt of her love for him and at the end she dies, like a queen and like a lover, for him and for him only:

> Methinks I hear
> Antony call; I see him rouse himself
> To praise my noble act.[4]

For many readers, from the very beginning to the end the theme of love eclipses all other themes. So much so that the play has been called "the apotheosis of sensual love" by Robert Ornstein, and T.S. Eliot is of the opinion:

> We are made to feel convinced of an overpowering attraction towards each other of two persons, not only in defiance of conventional morality, but against self-interest.[5]

Only the most important opinions in this respect will be discussed here. First of all there is Coleridge who, as has been pointed out above (*vide* Chap. 4 *supra*) couples it with *Romeo and Juliet*:

> This play should be perused in mental contrast with *Romeo and Juliet*—as the love of passion and appetite opposed to the love of affection and instinct.[6]

It is to be noted that both of these kinds of love exist in both the characters. It is not that Antony stands for the first kind of love and Cleopatra for the second or *vice versa*. Coleridge's viewpoint is more complex than such a simple classification would allow. He means that both of these kinds of love exist in both the characters, sometimes one coming to the surface and sometimes the other. He makes this clear in his remarks on the character of Cleopatra though he does not explain the point any further.

A.C. Bradley's view of the play as a love-tragedy has been discussed already (*vide* Chap. 3 *supra*). The very fact that he regards the play as a love-tragedy or romantic tragedy is an indication that he regards love as the central theme of the play. He rightly insists that the main effect of the tragedy depends upon the theme of intense love felt by the hero and the heroine for each other. We should not "deny the name of love to this ruinous passion". This is quite emphatically put.

Yet he gives us a very ambiguous interpretation of this love. His attitude to it is positive and yet in a sense it is negative also. First of all it is negative because this love is the cause of tragedy:

> It is plain that the love of Antony and Cleopatra is destructive...we sympathize with them in their passion.[7]

He stresses this negative quality of their love again and again, pointing out how the entire tragedy is based on this interplay, between the two characters, of love and anger, of loyalty and perfidy. This continues throughout the play.

But after this he gives a highly positive interpretation of this love. It is a love that commands our admiration and sympathy and which also exalts us because of its very nobility:

> We sympathize with them in their passion; we feel in it the infinity there is in man; even when we acquiesce in their defeat we are exulting in their victory.[8]

This exalting quality of their love brings him to another, a very serious, adverse criticism of the play. He regards the play as a failure because of this noble and exalted love. The spectators and the readers have the feeling that such a love looks upon the world and its wealth as nothing, that the two persons concerned are so rich in their love that they do not need imperial grandeur or wealth, that this love is more than enough in itself. So, when they die, we feel that they are not leaving anything that is precious—life itself or imperial grandeur:

> The greatness of Antony and Cleopatra in their fall is so much heightened by contrast with the world they lost and the conqueror who wins it, that the positive element in the final tragic impression, the element of reconciliation is strongly emphasized.[9]

Very much the same opinion is held by Una Ellis-Fermor (*vide* Chap. 3 *supra*). Antony is exalted by his love and all his other flaws are forgotten by us. The last stage of Cleopatra's life, known as her "ecstasy", also has the same effect:

> In the final act there is so much less of pain than in *Timon*, *Lear* or *Hamlet* that we hardly think of it as tragedy.[10]

This has become possible because of the elevated effect of the love they bear towards each other.

But this ennobling and elevating effect of love, as both of these critics have pointed out, mars the effect of tragedy. Tragedy, in order to be successful, must evoke the emotions of pity and terror. If, instead, we have a sense of fulfilment or of reconciliation or of the worthlessness of the world, then the tragic effect is seriously hampered, if not totally destroyed.

So it can be seen that the theme of love, which ennobles the characters also mars the tragic equilibrium of the play. This is a very serious flaw. As has been pointed out already (*vide* Chap. 3 *supra*) this is the case with *The Duchess of Malfi* and *Murder in the Cathedral* as well. There this feature is far more noticeable. When the Duchess of Malfi is killed we feel that she has gone straight to heaven and in *Murder in the Cathedral* we know, for sure, that Thomas a Becket is a holy martyr. It is emphasized in the choric song that follows. The effect is not so emphatic in the play under discussion. But there are quite a few critics who feel that the exaltation brought about by the intensity of love has marred tragic catharsis. Bradley holds this negative view. Other critics like Ellis-Fermor and Ornstein do not think of it as a defect but all the same they do point it out as one of the features of the theme of love.

(B) THEME OF SENSATION AS A DECEIT

It is true that Antony and Cleopatra live for, and also die for, love. Yet there exists the view that looks with strict moral rectitude upon this love itself and pronounces it to be highly negative by nature. It is self-evident that their love is destructive and has been pointed out to be so, but usually people consider this mutual attraction as love, not as something else. This is what Edward Dowden does. He denies it the name of love, particularly with reference to Cleopatra:

> We do not mistake this feeling of Cleopatra towards Antony for love; but he has been for her (who has known Caesar and Pompey) the supreme sensation.[11]

Antony is also known by all to be a voluptuary, a creature of sensation and, moreover, he is surrounded by a world of sensuous pleasure which gradually saps away his strength. Dowden, though he dwells more upon Cleopatra as a creature of sensation, does not let Antony go free either. Both of them are creatures of sensation, enjoying all the different sensations that unlimited wealth and power can give. Their life has been a story of continuous voluptuous self-indulgence.

According to Dowden Shakespeare deliberately holds up this image of a pair of voluptuous sensation-seeking lovers only in order to make us realize that this world of sensations is not an enduring one, that it is a world of deceit:

> What he seems to say to us in this play, not in the manner of a doctrinaire or a moralist, but wholly as an artist, is that this sensual infinite is but a dream, a deceit, a snare.[12]

This is a very important view of the theme of the play. Throughout the play one cannot help but be conscious of the excessive, the grandiose lifestyle of the imperial pair. Many legends have come down to us to the banquets they gave to each other. Much of this was accepted by their contemporaries and posterity as part of the imperial way of life, but there is no question that it used to be regarded as being excessive, it is not Dowden alone, who with strong Victorian morality, condemns it. Right in the beginning of the play disapproval is voiced by Philo who is one of his friends and later in Act I, sc. iv Octavius is no less scornful:

> he fishes, drinks and wastes
> The lamps of night in revel; is not more manlike
> Than Cleopatra.[13]

Misfortunes on the battlefield, betrayals, etc. have no effect on this sensuality. Both of them are so used to extravagant luxury that it has become natural for them. There is no one to criticise or contradict them and because both of them were of the same cast of mind there was no question of one of them controlling the other. So they lived a life of endless sensation-hunting.

Then the inevitable waning comes, ending in tragedy. This, according to Dowden is the theme of the play—this is what the poet wanted to convey to us, that this kind of life, this kind of love is an illusion, a trap. Shakespeare does not belittle the life led by the pair. Quite the opposite in fact—he emphasizes it whenever possible. There is the description of Cleopatra's barge of which "the poop was beaten gold" and the very sails were perfumed. Their love is such that it is beyond all reckoning, "There's beggary in the love that can be reckon'd." Everything is on a grandiose and excessive scale with them. By emphasizing this excessiveness Shakespeare makes the transitoriness of all this only more effective:

> The glory of the royal festival is not dulled by Shakespeare or diminished; but also he shows us in letters of flame the handwriting upon the wall.[14]

Both of them, ironically enough realize the deceit of which Dowden talks. For Antony the riches of the earth, the empire itself, become as nothing when he hears of Cleopatra's death:

> Now all labour
> Mars what it does, yea, very force entangles
> Itself with strength; seal then, and all is done.[15]

It is the same with Cleopatra. For her too the empire, the world itself, is worthless without him:

> Shall I abide
> In this dull world which in thy absence is
> No better than a sty?...
> ...young boys and girls
> Are level now with men; the odds is gone,
> And there is nothing left remarkable
> Beneath the visiting moon.[16]

It is when they are parting for ever from each other that the hollowness of the world becomes apparent. So perhaps, as Dowden points out, this is the theme that Shakespeare himself wanted to emphasize, though it is difficult to agree with Dowden when he says that their love cannot be called love. No other critic has said that it is a mistake to call it love.

(C) THE TRIUMPH OF TRANSCENDENTAL HUMANISM

An intensive study of the language and imagery in the play reveals that the ultimate end of the play is not justify or to punish two lovers, but to affirm a glorification of humanism, a "triumph of transcendental humanism." This is the view of

G. Wilson Knight which has been accepted and extended further by J. Middleton Murry.

This interpretation takes a philosophical and highly positive view of the play. The play has such spiritual and "visual imaginations" that it leaves the mundane day-to-day world behind. The story of two lovers and their downfall, the story of the Roman empire, all fade into insignificance and so does the "minor stressing of Antony's shame or disgrace". What triumphs at the end is the valiant human spirit that can rise above all misfortunes. He notes in detail such words and images as are evocative of power, of grandeur, of spiritual development and comes to this conclusion. Right at the end it is not Antony or Cleopatra, two human beings, who matter, but the spirit of humanity itself.

> Now we feel the pressure of our "mating" referred throughout, the constant stress on "melting", "dissolving", "mingling" till "strength" of eternity and "force" of time are inextricably "entangled".... In death man is triumphant, a "conqueror".[17]

The lines in which the most significant of the words quoted above by this critic occur will clarify what it is that he wants to say. The last three of the words given by him will amply illustrate his point. "Entangles" is one such significant word and it is spoken by Antony in a most moving speech:

> Now all labour
> Mars what it does; yea, very force entangles
> Itself with strength.[18]

Next comes the word "intrinsicate" spoken by Cleopatra. It is addressed to the asp:

> With thy sharp teeth this knot intrinsicate
> Of life at once untie.[19]

The last word cited by Wilson Knight is "conqueror" spoken by Antony about Cleopatra who by taking her own life proved to Octavius that he had no power over her. She cheated him of his triumph:

> Who by her death our Caesar tells
> "I am conqueror of myself."[20]

Each of these three quotations envisage man as noble, rising above the entanglements and intricacies of life to be conqueror over everything. This is what this critic calls "transcendental humanism" that triumphs over everything and has to be traced throughout the play in the very words and images used in it. This is a highly philosophical, not to say spiritual, interpretation of the theme of the play. John Middleton Murry takes it a step further, enriching the idea with further suggestions and analyses. Both of them are important critics and the view they advocate are likewise important. The diligent student will, however, not treat their views as exhaustive and definitive, for the method they have adopted is by no means a definitive one.

(D) THE VISION OF THE DIONYSIAC

Nietzsche, in his famous *The Birth of Tragedy* had given his views on the origins of tragedy as well as comedy. Basing his interpretation on the theory of Nietzsche, the modern critic M. Long has said that in *AC* we have a vision of the Dionysiac frenzy which includes a "comic wit":

> If we do not feel both the festal Laughter of Egyptian lyricism and the ribald laughter directed at Rome we shall read the play more solemnly than is required and miss the very essence of the vision of the Dionysiac which it has to impart.[21]

According to him the element of comedy is present in the play from the very beginning. He quotes Cleopatra's caricature of Octavius:

> Do this or this;
> Take in that kingdom and enfranchise that
> Perform't, or else we damn thee.[22]

Commenting on the note of comedy in these lines he says that this note will be kept throughout:

> These are the first notes of Dionysus' song, simultaneously lyrical and ribald, which will dominate the first half of the play and colour our view of Rome and Egypt.[23]

This comic element is to be found throughout the play, sometimes subdued and at other times loud and clear. This is not the only play in which such an element is to be found, for it is there in *Troilus and Cressida*, *Coriolanus* and *Henry IV* as well.

Before proceeding any further, one important point has to be clarified. It is a well-known fact that Elizabethan and Jacobean tragedies had the intermingling of tragedy and comedy in them and had been severely criticised by neo-classical critics, as this meant the violation of the Aristotelian unity of action. This element of comic relief however is quite different from the kind of comedy that has been found in the play by this critic. The comic relief as present in these plays had been introduced in separate comic scenes and is recognized as providing relief from tragic tension in the plays. It is pure and simple comedy and most of the time it had very little to do with the tragic action. That kind of comedy is to be found in this play also and will be discussed in the proper place later (*vide* Chap. 8, *infra*). The Dionysiac song that the present critic is talking about is far more subtle an element and is more integrally related to the play. It can hardly be separated from the play as a scene set apart. It is permeated throughout the play in attitude, diction and imagery. Moreover, it has a satirical touch about it, satirising the established Roman rule:

> The ribald, anti-imperial comedy of *Troilus and Cressida* and *Henry IV* has contributed a great deal to the portrayal of Rome in *Antony and Cleopatra*.[24]

So the caricature of Octavius given by Cleopatra is anti-imperialistic satire which is typical of Dionysiac irreverence towards all kind of power and politics.

But Dionysus or Bacchus is the god of wine and revelry as well and this aspect of Dionysiac revelry is to be found in the frequent feasts and banquets that take place in the play. This is mostly an Egyptian feature whereas the satirical part is mostly Roman and anti-imperialistic:

> ...on the other hand the comedy of lyric delight and love-play is given to the Egyptian part of the play, a Bacchic romanticism.[25]

These two different attitudes have been named by this critic as "the comedy of delicate derision" and "the comedy of festival and pleasure".

As a matter of fact both of these attitudes are so much a part of the play that it is not possible to separate them. But it is mostly in the first half of the play that anti-imperialist satire is to be found. There are repeated references to Rome and her heroes that are all derogatory ones. It "is seen with airy and scurrilous comedy as absurd." Cleopatra finds Caesar and Pompey to be "Paltry and absurd." Caesar is a "scarce-bearded" boy who talks pompously and thinks himself to be very important and grand. This pomposity and self-importance and formality amuse the Egyptian contingent. There are always "ripples of mirthful disbelief" in *AC* which are communicated to the reader. A detailed analysis of the play from this point of view is not necessary here. The self-important pomposity of Rome is repeatedly juxtaposed to the merriment and revelry of Egypt to the former's denigration. What this critic calls "Rome's deflation by laughter" is seen again and again at its most obvious in the banquet scene:

Enob. There is a strong fellow, Menas.

(pointing to the servant who carries off Lepidus)

Men. Why?

Eno. A bears the third part of the world, man, see'st not?[26]

There is even a song to Bacchus in this scene, which is the only song in the whole play.

Even in the second half of the play the "vision of the Dionysiac" is to be found again and again, but here it is the romanticism of the vision that predominates. There is laughter, grotesquerie, ribaldry, sensual excitement, all rolled into one:

> In *AC* the whole tangle of Dionysiac elements can only be taken as being of a piece, the whole chaos of it all taken as it is in the certain knowledge, imparted by this great romanticism, that without these grotesqueries there will be no creature life.[27]

This is a novel and significant view of the play, but it must not be confused with the concept of comic relief and unity of action.

(E) A PSYCHOLOGICAL MORASS

Kay Stockholder, a critics who uses the psychoanalytical method to interpret *AC* gives it as her considered opinion that *AC*:

> *AC* invites us into the psychological morass that underlies the seduction of love-death romance.[28]

She points out that Antony had had no parental figure to admonish and control him, or anyone else who would take their place:

> He inhabits a world free of parents or paternally symbolized power relations.[29]

With this as her starting point this critic goes on the argue that as Antony is under no compulsion to obtain parental approval for his relationship with Cleopatra, therefore unconsciously he has but the Roman characters, and army and citizens, in a word Rome itself in their place, investing them in his mind with parental authority and the power to criticize him. He is not aware of these deep waters within himself, but Cleopatra is. He refuses to see the Roman ambassador and she is acute enough to know, or rather make a guess at, the reason:

> Cleopatra's implied accusation that Antony on her account feels diminished in Roman eyes and thereby gives parental force to Caesar and the militaristic approval he represents.[30]

Indeed, in the very first scene Cleopatra makes this quite clear when Antony refuses to give audience to the messenger from Rome:

> Your dismission
> Is come from Caesar, therefore hear it, Antony,
> Thou blushest, Antony, and that blood of thine
> Is Caesar's homager; else so thy cheek pays shame
> When shrill-tongu'd Fulvia scolds.[31]

Rome, for Antony, stands for maturity and authority and he can himself attain to that state only by forgoing his love-life with Cleopatra. Indeed, Shakespeare makes it quite clear that Roman life is one of discipline and hard-headed realism, not of the luxurious romanticism that Egyptian Life stands for. Yet paradoxically it is to a Roman woman that he's is legitimately married, not once but twice. They are the ones who can provide him with legitimate heirs to carry on the tasks of a triumvir. He has already left Fulvia who, as Cleopatra says, is "Shrill-tongu'd" and who scolds. Her death becomes known in the first scene. The next woman he marries is Octavia, which marriage is again a loveless one, made for political reasons:

> I will to Egypt;
> And though I make this marriage for my peace,
> I' the east my pleasure lies.[32]

Octavia is a loyal wife and a person of great rectitude but she can never say, like Cleopatra:

> Eternity was in our lips and eyes,
> Bliss in our brows bent.[33]

So he has to placate Rome with its disapproval and strong moral viewpoint if he wants to attain maturity. But a kind of immaturity accompanied by a sense of guilt is present in his intense but illegitimate relationship with Cleopatra.

This theme is carried on throughout the play and when Antony comes to know in Act III: sc. vii that Caesar has already arrived and is ready to give battle he looks upon himself as being deprived of martial powers. The Soothsayer has already told him to stay away from Caesar, for Caesar's star is in the ascendant. Then comes the episode of unearthly music that is heard at night by the soldiers. This music is interpreted by them as signifying the departure of Hercules whose favour Antony had gained. All these things combine to convince Antony that he is going to he punished for his illegitimate and immoral love-affair with Cleopatra:

> This scene shows Antony divesting himself of his martial powers and translating them into a supernaturally punitive paternal force...he manages to defy a paternal witness, when he claims a maternal Cleopatra and simultaneously punishes himself for this oedipal crime.[34]

This kind of psychoanalytical analysis sheds a new light on the work it deals with, but it should be accepted with reservations.

There are many other themes that have been found in the play. Only a few of them have been discussed above. Besides these there is what Coleridge has called "love of passion and appetite opposed to the love of affection and instinct", "the fall of the world-republic" as given by Georg Brandes, "torments of love and the incompatibility of politics and private desire" given by Franklin Dickey, "impulse of a heightened sense of Life and fulfilment" given by L.C. Knights and many more. The great complexity of Shakespeare's plays can be judged from this variety of opinions. What seems to be a simple historical tragedy is seen to have numerous themes. Those that have been discussed or mentioned here are treated as the central themes of the play. Besides these there are many sub-themes adding to the rich complexity of the play.

REFERENCES

1. Fluchère, Henri, *Shakespeare,* London, Longmans, Green & Co., 1953, p. 195.
2. Act IV, sc. x, lines 44-47.
3. IV : viii : 60-62.
4. V : ii : 285-87.
5. Eliot, T.S., *Elizabethan Dramatists,* London, Faber & Faber, Ltd., 1963, p. 125.
6. Coleridge in Brown J.R. *op. cit.*, p. 29.
7. *Ibid.*, p. 75.
8. *Ibid.*, pp. 75-76.
9. *Ibid.*, p. 74.
10. Ellis-*Fermor, ii, op. cit.,* p. 267.
11. Dowden, E. in Brown, J.R. *op. cit.*, p. 41.
12. *Ibid.*
13. I : iv : 4-6.
14. Dowden, E., *op. cit.,* p. 41.
15. IV : xii : 47-49.
16. IV : xiii : 60-68.
17. Knight, G. Wilson, *The Imperial Theme*, London, 1932, p. 262.
18. IV : xii : 47-49.

19. V: ii : 306-07.
20. IV : xii : 61-62.
21. Long, M., *Antony and Cleopatra and the Song of Dionysus* in Brown, J.R. *op. cit.*, p. 180.
22. I : i : 22-24.
23. Brown, J.R. *op. cit.*, p. 171.
24. *Ibid.*, pp. 171-72.
25. *Ibid.*, p. 172.
26. II : vii : 87-89
27. Long, M., *op. cit.*, p. 184.
28. Stockholder, Kay, in Brown, J.R. *op. cit.*, p. 204.
29. *Ibid.*, p. 192.
30. *Ibid.*, p. 193.
31. I : i : 26-32.
32. II : iii : 38-39.
33. I : iii : 35-36.
34. Stockholder, Kay, *op. cit.*, p. 195.

6

The Major Characters

(A) SHAKESPEARE'S CHARACTERS

Shakespeare has added more figures to the gallery of dramatic characters than any other dramatist. As it is, his characters are a class by themselves. Critics and readers have stood amazed at the profusion and complexity of his characters. They are not only lifelike and realistic—that is only the beginning. They are also universal and often have symbolic implications.

It is not that the other dramatics of his time did not give us great and memorable characters. Marlowe, Webster, Ben Jonson, have all created great characters. But on the other hand, they spent their energies over the main characters, to the neglect of minor ones. Not so with our poet, for his minor characters are never shadowy ones, lacking individuality. This creates the impression of a well-populated background against which the major characters play their roles. It is not that there is one overwhelming titanic figure against which all the other appear to be like flitting shadows.

A very important point about Shakespeare's creativity is that he never stood still but went on developing till the last. His art went on reaching different levels of maturity and so did his art of character portrayal. It is not for nothing that Dryden comparing his characters with those of Ben Jonson, has said in the *Prologue* to *Julius Caesar*:

> The faultless Jonson equally writ well,
> Shakespeare made faults, but then did more excel.
>
> ... ...

> In Imitation, Jonson's wit was shown,
> Heaven made his men, but Shakespeare made his own![1]

Like his other techniques, that of character-portrayal, too, developed gradually. The two pairs of lovers in *A Midsummer Night's Dream*, for example, are not very clearly distinguished from each other and it is a surprising fact that the humble weaver Bottom, is a far more remarkable person than the noble Duke Theseus.

As his apprenticeship is left behind his characters become more and more distinctive. There are the important figures of the Chronicle plays with Falstaff gaining not just pre-eminence but uniqueness, and the heroines of the golden Comedies. These latter are so well-portrayed that they overshadow the heroes. It is a paradoxical fact that the only male figure to gain overwhelming importance, leaving even the romantic heroes far beneath him is the villain, Shylock who makes the heroes pale into insignificance. Bottom, Falstaff, Shylock are all of them most unexpected characters to gain such power.

It is in the third stage of his career that the great male figures make their appearance. The great tragic figures come in the tragedies and the problem comedies. Here, indeed, he produced more than lifesize figures who are much more than merely realistic once. One does not wonder that Pope says:

> His characters are so much more than Nature herself that 'tis a sort of injury to call them by so distant a name as copies of her.[2]

But his character-drawing would go a further kind of change in the Last Romances. Now his concern is no longer the existence of evil as it was in the tragedies and the problem comedies. Instead he has become interested in man's reaction to it, the different ways of tackling it. Sin is unavoidable, but it can lead to repentance and thence to purification. The dramatist shows his heroes undergoing spiritual development along this path to emerge chastened, forgiven and forgiving, at the end. They are succeeded by a purer and younger generation to continue the process of life. Such figures are not merely universal, but ascend to a higher level, attaining to the status of the symbolic.

These are but some of the qualities that elevate his characters above the level of those of the others—and this in spite of the fact that in most of the cases they are not his own individual independent creation. As will be seen in a later Chapter (*vide* Chap. 8 Plot *infra*) he took his stories from plays and tales that already existed from before. But they had been, most of them, sketched in a perfunctory manner. He was the one who gave them flesh and blood, individuality and existence. In the present case the characters are colourful historical figures, specially the ones of the hero and the heroine. Shakespeare already had a firm foundation here to work upon and gave them renewed vitality.

It must not, however, be forgotten that he had to work, in every instance, according to certain rules and conventions, contemporary as well as classical ones. He accepted and followed the rules, but always made use of them in such a way as to enhance his own creations:

> It is equally undeniable that, allowing for his own peculiar genius, he conforms with the accepted conventions of character-drawing as with other conventions.[3]

It is a remarkable fact that the guidelines he followed were the same as were available to the other dramatists, yet no one created such characters. The classical rules that were followed were the ones that had been laid down by Aristotle and Horace and had been explained and commented upon by Italian scholars later. He had already studied Seneca's tragedies and the comedies of Plautus and Terence in school, so there was no dearth of examples. In addition to these, several works had been written by Elizabethan writers themselves. These gave the theories about character-portrayal as well as examples. A few of them are: Newton's *The Touchstone of Complexions*, Bishop Hall's *Characters of Virtues and Vices,* Sir Thomas Overbury's *Characters*, etc. These were available to everyone, but not everyone was able to create a Hamlet or a Lear or a Rosalind out of them. The magic pen of Shakespeare was the only thing to perform that miracle.

(B) THE CLASSICAL RULES

The tradition of writing character-sketches goes back to Aristotle. He had given long and detailed descriptions of six different types of characters in his *Nichomachaean Ethics*. It became the fashion thereafter to add to this list. Theophrastus, whose work was available in translation, could give a list of a hundred characters by the end of the Renaissance. Quintilian had called these sketches "set definitions of fixed characters". In his *Poetics* Aristotle had given certain rules that applied to all characters and the later writers followed these rules. There are four of them: (a) Proportion, (b) Appropriateness, (c) Realism, and (d) Consistency. These will be explained briefly now.

(a) Proportion

This attribute is also translated as Goodness as the term has a deeply moral implication. Aristotle has said that the motivation of a character must be a good one:

> Any speech or action that manifests moral purpose of any kind will be expressive of character : the character will be good if the purpose is good.[4]

This is not as simplistic as it sounds. Aristotle was a very scrupulous writer, looking at every aspect of any statement or fact. So he points out that goodness depends on the social level of the characters. He gives the following example: if a servant does not steal from his master he is good, but the same cannot be said about a gentleman whose social level and standard are both different. Shakespeare excels in portraying this trait. In the play that is being studied all the characters are historical ones, yet even here he has observed this Aristotelian rule. Bullough has pointed out in this connection:

> What Shakespeare learned from Plutarch was to represent more clearly than before the paradoxes of human motives, the mixture of good and evil in the same person.[5]

(b) Appropriatness

The second requirement for a dramatic character as given by Aristotle is Appropriateness or Propriety. A character should act or speak according to his inherent nature. He points out:

> There is a type of manly valour; but valour in a woman or unscrupulous cleverness is inappropriate.[6]

Shakespeare's characters never speak or act in any way that is not in keeping with their nature. A very good example of this is Pompey's refusal to accept the advice of Menas. It is completely in keeping with the nobility of his nature to refuse to kill his guests. The same can be said about Antony when he sends Enobarbus the treasure that was due to him even after coming to know that Enobarbus has deserted him for Caesar. It is like him to be so noble.

(c) Realism

Realism is the third quality and Aristotle has not written much about it. He just says that a character should be true to life and points out that it is different from goodness and propriety. Shakespeare's expertise in this respect can hardly be rivalled by anybody else. M.C. Bradbrook lays special stress upon this skill:

> Shakespeare's innovations in Character-drawing may be compared to the introduction of perspective in painting: he gave the illusion of life.[7]

(d) Consistency

Consistency is the fourth requirement in character-portrayal. This is the most important of all, and it means that a character should be true to itself and remain so without any sudden and unacceptable changes. It must be acknowledged that there are certain cases of a sudden, drastic change of heart in our poet as there is in many Elizabethan plays. He was a poet, a creator, and he could and did, follow rules or neglect then according to his own will or convenience. Pope had said, with the assurance of a poet himself:

> To judge therefore of Shakespeare by Aristotle's rules is like trying a man by the laws of one country, who acted under those of another.[8]

The four traits discussed above are applicable to dramatic characters in general. In addition to these there are some others for the tragic hero. Shakespeare had, in addition to these theoretical rules, the practical examples of Seneca among the classics and those of Kyd, Marlowe and other English dramatists, to help him.

The rules given by Aristotle, in addition to the four already given above, and meant especially for the tragic hero are: the tragic hero must be better than the average; he must have some kind of flaw or shortcoming in his nature. This last is the most important. The Elizabethans understood it as the tragic flaw which brings doom and destruction upon the hero. Aristotle took care to point out that it is not a serious moral flaw:

> A man who is not eminently good and just, yet whose misfortune is brought about not by vice or depravity but by some error or frailty.[9]

The term for this "error of judgement" that he uses is *hamartia*. This error of judgement, in later plays came to mean a serious flaw in the hero's character, as for example ambition in Macbeth, jealousy in Othello, etc. It need not, however, be so destructive for a much less serious flaw will be enough to mar the nobility of a hero without seriously imperilling his dignity. Aristotle is careful to preserve the nobility and insists that the hero must be superior to the average man:

> Tragedy is an imitation of persons who are above the common level.... The poet, in representing men who are irascible or indolent, or have such other defects of character, should present the type and yet ennoble it.[10]

The character of Antony is truly that of an ideal tragic hero from the Aristotelian view.

When we start considering the characters of the play under discussion, one thing should always be kept in kind: these are well-known historical figures, just as in the English chronicle plays. In both of these plays the poet had to follow the account given by the historians, Plutarch in the present case. This must have presented quite a challenge to his artistic ability, for he had to keep to the historically known facts and opinions and create a living character out of them. J.I.M. Stewart has put this problem in a succint manner. According to him there are two distinct levels or "planes" in these historical plays:

> ...The planes upon which Shakespeare builds : the simple outward and heroic plane upon which men show themselves to the world like figures on a stage; and the complex and inward plane along which we are drawn to a knowledge of the hidden man.[11]

Horace has something very relevant to say in this respect. He is writing here about the Homerian character Achilles, but what he says applies to the present case in a most fitting manner:

> Either follow the beaten track, or invent something that is consistent within itself. If in your play you happen to be representing the illustrious Achilles, let him he energetic, passionate, ruthless and implacable.[12]

In other words he takes the example of Achilles to clarify what the dramatist has to do if he is depicting a well-known figure. The principle he outlines will apply to the characters in *AC*. Our dramatist has followed both the principles given by Horace. He "follows the beaten track" in being true to the picture presented by Plutarch and also does he "invent something that is consistent within itself." This, moreover, is done with such great psychological and artistic insight that the characters emerge as both historically true and realistically acceptable.

The characters in *AC* are now to be considered individually. Usually, in a tragedy, it is the hero's character that is the first to be considered and often, as in Marlowe, the only one of real importance. In this play however, the heroine is of equal importance. Several critics have pointed out that in historical plays the attention need not be focused on a single hero. Moreover, it is difficult in such cases to dissociate the characters from history and judge them independently:

> ...we often have such difficulties with Shakespeare's historical characters, reading into them extraneous matters and distorting the significance of his text. To Shakespeare the love of Antony and Cleopatra was no mere vulgar liaison between the sensualist conqueror and a royal trull... To Shakespeare the all important thing was the personality of his characters.[13]

(C) MARK ANTONY

Antony the tragic hero is the most important male character in the play. In comparison with him the other male characters seem to be diminutive figures. The most glorified description of his personality is given by Cleopatra in the last Act of the play during her ecstasy and the least glorified descriptions are given by Philo and Octavius in the first Act. A like ambivalence exists in the minds of the critics and this has been the case from the very beginning. This can be understood the best from what A.W. Schlegel says:

> In Antony we observe a mixture of great qualities, weaknesses and vices; violent ambitions and ebullitions of magnanimity.[14]

Entirely derogatory remarks on him hardly exist as also there is a dearth of entirely appreciative ones. This fact in itself shows how well Shakespeare has observed the rule of Proportion as given by Aristotle. Not only Antony's own contemporaries but posterity, who have judged him on Shakespear's portrayal are equally bemused. They do not seem to be able to make up their minds to give a balanced judgement.

Shakespeare presents various aspects of his character: as a lover, as a warrior, a statesman, etc., and every aspect is presented in a positive as well as a negative manner. Thus on his very first appearance he establishes himself as an ardent and extravagant lover:

> *Ant.* There's beggary in the love that can be reckon'd
>
> *Cl.* I'll set a bourne how far to be belov'd
>
> *Ant.* Then must thou needs find out new heaven, new earth.[15]

As a lover he has been portrayed again, in an ambivalent manner. First of all his love is immoral, adulterous, and this has been pointed out by the earliest critics, with Dryden calling both of them "patterns of unlawful love".

He is a sensual man and this side of his nature is satisfied by Cleopatra and by nobody else. That is the reason he is bound to her by fetters stronger than those of iron and he realizes it only too well. It is an enervating love, a love that has deprived him of his status as a hero:

These strong Egyptian fetters I must break
Or lose myself in dotage.
... ...
I must from enchanting queen break off;
Ten thousand harms, more than the ills I know
My idleness doth hatch.[16]

Thus he is quite conscious of his emotional slavery to Cleopatra, yet he cannot give her up, even though everyone in Rome disapproves of it. He agrees to marry Octavia, knowing full well that he will not be able to give her his love—it is a marriage of convenience. Even in the same scene in which he meets Octavia and promises her he will not break the rules in future, he determines that he will go back to Cleopatra:

I will to Egypt;
And though I make this marriage for my peace,
I' the east my pleasure lies.[17]

It is because of this love of his that he is defeated in the battle of Actium. Cleopatra fled the place in a cowardly manner and he followed her in a most shameful manner "Like a doting mallard." He knew full well that it was a thoroughly shameful betrayal on her part and yet he forgave her. This has been praised as a noble action, for his love for her has been regarded as an all-compensating factor:

Fall out a tear, I say; one of them rates
All that is won and lost. Give me a kiss;
Even this repays me.[18]

The glorification of love is seen at its best when he comes to know of Cleopatra's death. The relevant lines have already been quoted a few times. Without her life is worthless to him and he gives her the best thing he can give her, his life itself. What more is there for a man to give?

I will be
A bridegroom in my death, and run into't
As to a lover's bed.[19]

Even after his attempt at suicide has failed and he comes to know that Cleopatra had merely told him a lie, his love does not wane;

> I am dying, Egypt, dying; only
> I here importune death awhile until
> Of many thousand kisses the poor last
> I lay upon thy lips.[20]

It is after his death that the portrait of his unqualified and undoubted greatness is given by Cleopatra. To her women first and again later to Dolabella she ecstatically describes him as a titan:

> His face was as the heavens and therein stuck
> A sun and moon, which kept their course and lighted
> The little O, the earth...
> For his bounty
> There was no winter in it, an autumn't was
> That grew the more by reaping.[21]

This sentence about his bounty is perfectly true. The best example of it is to be seen when he sends Enobarbus all his wealth and more, even after knowing that the latter has deserted him for Caesar. What better example of bounty can ever be found when he does not even blame Enobarbus?

All this and much more, can be said about Antony as a lover. There is no less diversity of opinion about him as a soldier. Here there is great difference between the Antony of pre-Cleopatra days and the Antony of now. In fact this is the main reason why persons like Philo, Octavius and others have become so contemptuous of him. In the very first speech Philo says:

> His captain's heart,
> Which in the scuffles of great fights hath burst
> The buckles on his breast, reneges all temper[22]

He retains his courage and valour, but his infatuation has robbed him of his judgement as a warrior. First of all, he decides to fight at sea in spite of being advised to the contrary. Moreover, it is quite clear that he does this out of sheer unreasoning obstinacy:

> *Ant.* By sea, by sea.
>
> *Eno.* Most worthy sir, you therein throw away
> The absolute soldiership you have by land...
>
> *Ant.* I'll fight at sea.[23]

This is bad enough. But much worse follows when in the battle of Actium Cleopatra betrays him by withdrawing her navy at a crucial point during the fight and he follows her, leaving his navy without a leader:

She once being loof'd,
The noble ruin of her magic, Antony
Claps on his sea-wing, and like a doting mallard
Leaving the fight in height, flies after her.
I never saw an action of such shame,
Experience, manhood, honour, ne'er before
Did violate so itself.[24]

Yet, even after this shameful exhibition Antony is again reinstated in his martial glory when he wins the fight in the Three Days' Battle:

he hath fought today
As if a god, in hate of mankind, had
Destroy'd in such a shape.[25]

But after this comes the final defeat when he is betrayed once more by Cleopatra. Yet he attains to a titanic status in these last lines when, betrayed and defeated, he still manages to cheat Octavius of his triumph by killing himself:

Not Caesar valor hath o'erthrown Antony
But Antony's hath triumph'd on itself.[26]

Thus throughout the play Antony has been portrayed as a great and noble here, but like all such tragic heroes, he too has many ups and downs in his nature. Hazlitt expressed it the best when he wrote about "the irregular grandeur of the soul of Mark Antony".

From the classical point of view he can easily be called the ideal tragic hero. All the requirements of such a hero are to be found in him. Apart from the obvious points like his being nobly born, noble by nature and being present on the stage in the maximum number of scenes, the four qualities mentioned above are all present in him. The fact that his "grandeur" is "irregular" as Hazlitt had said, proves that the quality of Proportion is eminently present in him. His action and speeches are both appropriate to his station in life. Even when, lost to all sense of shame, he followed Cleopatra at Actium, it is appropriate as the action of an absolutely infatuated lover. The only criticism that can be levelled against him is that he is lacking in the virtue of consistency, as he goes on changing his attitude as a lover and as a warrior again and again. But here it can be said that he is true to what Aristotle had pointed out, that even if a character appears to be inconsistent, "still he must be consistently inconsistent".[27] Thus, when he appears to be changing his standpoint and his opinion, he is still being true, or consistent, to himself.

As for the all-important trait of *hamartia* there is no need to search for it, as it is present from the very beginning, from the very first words he utters, to the end of the play, the very last words he utters. It is his love for Cleopatra. This point has already been discussed under the topics of genre—the play as a love-tragedy, and the theme of love (*vide* Chaps. 4 and 5, *supra*). It is his love that has ruined him and it is that which has, paradoxically, exalted him as well. It is this that has brought about the gradual degeneration in this character that brought about his tragic doom:

> Antony is daily dropping away from all that is sound, strong and enduring. His judgement wanes and his fortune.[28]

Thus, when all is said and done, he remains a tragic hero, splendid in his isolation, like *Othello*, *Hamlet*, *Macbeth* and many others.

(D) CLEOPATRA

She is one of the most important female characters of Shakespeare—it is a well-acknowledged fact. The simple fact that in a tragedy she gets equal prominence with the hero is proof enough. There is another feature that distinguishes her as a tragic figure: in *Romeo and Juliet*, Juliet gets nearly equal importance with Romeo, but her death is more pathetic than tragic, and the effect of her death is not only counterbalanced by that of Romeo, but also by the feigned death she had undergone earlier. Lady Macbeth is a very important character, but the tragedy is less hers than Macbeth's. Cleopatra however dies like a queen and her death is in no way minimized by that of Antony. Moreover, Antony dies in Act IV and entire Act V, the last and the most important Act of a tragedy, is devoted entirely to her. It is in that Act that she gains her tragic stature.

As is the case with Antony, she too has been judged by critics in a manner strictly moral as well as with great indulgence. Dryden had looked upon her and Antony as "famous patterns of unlawful love," and Hazlitt had said:

> She is voluptuous, ostentatious, conscious, boastful of her charms, haughty, tyrannical, fickle...Octavia is a dull foil to her.[29]

In the play itself she has been called many abusive names: "strumpet," "royal trull," "gipsy," etc. But, on the other hand there are ecstatic descriptions of her also, by critics as well as the persons in the play, best expressed by Bradley:

> Many unpleasant things can be said of Cleopatra, and the more that are said the more wonderful she appears.[30]

As for positive opinions about her in the play itself, the best, of course, is that of Enobarbus:

> Age cannot wither her, nor custom stale
> Her infinite variety; other women cloy
> The appetite they feed, but she makes hungry
> Where must she satisfies.[31]

She has been blamed, among other things, for having caused Antony's ruin. But it is not that she has caused only his ruin, but her own also. A.W. Schlegel, indeed, has expressed it the best:

> As they die for each other, we forgive
> them for having lived for each other.[32]

Her capriciousness, her acuteness, her passion, all are clearly demonstrated in the very first scene when she enters the stage. It is she who, with more instinctive knowledge of statecraft than Antony, persuades him to see the messenger from Rome. In fact she insists on it and will not let him rest till he has done so. When after seeing not one, but two of them he enters, she is angry and jealous. She accuses him of wanting to go to

Rome because his wife Fulvia wants it. Then the minute she hears of Fulvia's death, instead of being pleased at the news she accuses Antony of not feeling sad about it and says he will not miss her, either, when she dies.

> Now I see, I see,
> In Fulvia's death, how mine received shall be.[33]

The news of Antony's marriage to Octavia brings out the virago in her. It is the worst picture of her that has been given by the poet. She is absolutely uncontrolled and behaves like a demented fishwife. She abuses the messenger, hits him and threatens to kill him also.

> *Cie.*: The most infectious pestilence upon thee!
> (She strikes him down)
> *Mess.*: Good madam, patience.
> *Cie.*: What say you? Hence
> (Strikes him again),
> Horrible villain! or I'll spurn thine eyes
> Like balls before me; I'll unhair thy head.
> (She hales him up and down)
> Rogue, thou hast liv'd too long
> (Draws a knife)[34]

This terrifying and extremely vulgar exhibition of temper like that of a spoilt child is repulsive enough but the later interview with the same messenger is worse. There she is fully controlled but she show a lamentable want of judgement along with a credulousness that would be disgusting if it were not so ridiculous. In fact the scene has to be treated as a comic one. It is the same messenger who has come and he has learnt not to say the truth but to say what will please her. He is a very clever man and says what he feels will please her the most. From her very questions he can make out what kind of answer she wants to hear: It is quite a long passage and only his answers are being given below. The questions can be easily guessed at. She wants to know everything about Octavia: her looks, nature, everything:

> Madam, I heard her speak; she is low-voic'd
> ... ...
> She creeps
> Her motion and her station are as one;
> ... ...
> She was a widow...
> And I do think, she's thirty.
> ... ...
> Round even to faultiness
> ... ...
> Brown madam, and her forehead
> As low as she would wish it.[35]

All this about Octavia who was a noted beauty. So he pleases Cleopatra and gets gold in return, but we cannot praise her here. The whole scene is a comic one because of her gullibility. She believes all that the messenger says because that is what she wants to believe. But she should know that people hardly ever tell the truth to kings and queens, specially because this is a man she had formerly abused and threatened. Yet she never suspects him of telling lies and rests secure in the knowledge that Octavia is unattractive physically as well as mentally. She never thinks of verifying the messenger's words—she does not want to.

Later when she meets Antony after having betrayed him in the battle of Actium. She is humble and asks pardon, taking the full burden of responsibility on her own shoulders as indeed she ought to. But then, she is not frightened by Antony who is sorrowful rather than angry. At this point, it is easy to sympathize with her and approve of her attitude, because she admits that she is wrong.

Then after Antony has recovered himself and is victorious in the battle that was to continue and ultimately end in his defeat, she betrays him again and this time Antony is truly angry because he realizes that this is his final defeat. She too realizes that this anger besides being fully justified will not yield easily into forgiveness. So she uses a ploy that is going to bring ruin upon both of them. Antony had said much earlier in the play that she is a very cunning woman ("she is cunning past man's thought"). This cunning now shows itself when she retires into the monument and sends him a message that she has committed suicide. She never dreams of the disastrous results this falsehood might produce. This time she has finally overreached herself in her artfulness. She knows Antony will forgive and forget everything when he hears of her death, and he does exactly that. His state of mind is, as Bradley has pointed out, very like that of the writer of the dark lady sonnets and of Troilus:

> If the sonnets about the dark lady were, as need not be doubted, in some degree autobiographical, Shakespeare may well have used his personal experience both when he drew Cressida and when he drew Cleopatra.[36]

It is in the last scene of this Act, with Antony's death, that she begins to attain tragic status. Shakespeare has given her some of his best poetry. Indeed from this time onwards she speaks some of the maturest and most memorable passages in Shakespeare, which have already been quoted earlier. This entire part from here till her death has come to be known as "Cleopatra's ecstasy."

It is not that her tragic dignity stands unimpaired till the end. There is a significant moment when there is a lapse from it. This occurs when she gives a false inventory of her possessions to Caesar, and not, as many think, when she kneels down to him in humble submission. Though she is kneeling and submitting to his rule she does not lose in dignity. This humility, paradoxically, elevates her, enhancing her tragic status. But when she gives the false list, then indeed does she appear to be rather small. This meanness is not worthy of a great queen, specially when she affirms it to be a true one. Such falsehood is most undignified. But after this, preparing for death, she regains tragic dignity and greatness:

> Give me my robe, put on my crown, I have
> Immortal longings in me; now no more.
> The juice of Egypt's grape shall moist this lip.[37]

Iras is already dead and Charmian too dies after her. When Caesar enters it is to find them all dead. And his awestruck comment on her beauty and majesty is well-known. It is, as a matter of fact, one of the most oft-quoted descriptions of her:

> As she would catch another Antony
> In her strong toil of grace.[38]

No other female character in Shakespeare has been invested with so much grandeur and so much majesty. Dowden's remark, after 150 years, is still relevant:

> In her death there is something dazzling and splendid, something sensuous, something theatrical, something magnificently coquettish, nothing stern.[39]

(E) OCTAVIUS CAESAR

Though, after Antony and Cleopatra all the other characters seem to be unimportant and dwarf-like, yet due importance should be given to Octavius, also called Caesar in this play. He is one of the triumvirs and it will so happen that after the death of Antony he will be the only one left to be the Emperor of what was to become the Roman Empire. He is the great-nephew and adopted son of Julius Caesar and became known later as Emperor Augustus. Here, however, he has not yet attained to that stature. It is Antony's defeat and death which will bring him his later glory.

In the play itself both Antony and Cleopatra refer to him all the time in a contemptuous manner, nor has he fared much better in the hands of the literary critics who, most of the time, just neglect him. Bradley makes the position clear:

> Shakespeare, I think, took little interest in the character of Octavius and he has not made it wholly clear.[40]

Antony and Cleopatra mock at him much before he appears in the play, specially Cleopatra. Her caricature of him is quite well-known. She calls him "scarce-bearded Caesar", yet all the same she knows his importance in the Roman world and persuades Antony to see his messenger. We see him first in the fourth scene of the first Act. He shows himself as a cold, calculating statesman. Bradley's view of what Shakespeare thought of him is very important in this connection:

> To Shakespeare he was one of those men, like Bolingbroke and Ulysses, who have plenty of "judgement" and

> not much "blood". Victory in the world, according to the poet, almost always goes to such men, and he makes us respect, fear and dislike them.[41]

He impresses us at his very first appearance with his moral rectitude and contempt for Antony. This is all the more formidable as he is ready to concede a minor love-affair or illicit relationship, but not the all-consuming passion of Antony. This naturally makes one suspect that perhaps it is because he himself is cold, unswayed by passion, that he cannot understand genuine passion:

> Let us grant it is not
> Amiss to tumble on the bed of Ptolemy,
> To give a kingdom for a mirth...
> ...but to confound such time
> That drums him from his sport...
> ...'tis to be child
> As we rate boys.[42]

Yet it is also clear that he has deep respect for Antony, the warrior that he is. As soon as he hears of Pompey's advancing army he cries out to the absent Antony how much he wants him:

> Leave thy lascivious wassails. When thou once
> Was beaten from Modena...
> ...whom thou fought against
> Tho' daintily brought up, with patience more
> Than savages could suffer.[43]

This entire speech is a more valuable tribute to Antony the soldier, the warrior, the hero than the wonderful passages by Cleopatra. Octavius knows the martial valour of Antony, though he can never approve of Antony the lover as indeed no Roman could. It is left for literary critics to appreciate Antony the lover who can give up the world for love Octavius's attitude is quite in character. It can be taken to exemplify all the four requirements given by Aristotle: Proportion, Appropriateness, Realism and Consistency.

After this is Act II, sc. ii when Antony has come to Rome he treats him with dignity, as an equal, not bowing down to him. He does not scruple to point out his shortcomings which, indeed, are many. Antony acknowledges the fact that he has truly been remiss in his duties as a ruler, a Triumvir and this proves that he acknowledges Octavius's importance, however much he might have scorned him in Egypt. The quarrel between them could have had serious consequences, for Octavius shows himself in an unbending mood as he hurls one accusation after another at Antony. As soon as Agrippa proposes the marriage of his sister Octavia with Antony he at once realizes the feasibility of the proposal. Here he clearly shows his acumen as a politician:

> A sister I bequeath you, whom no brother
> Did ever love so dearly; let her live
> To join our kingdoms and our hearts.[44]

He does not speak much in the banquet scene, but it is to be noted that it is he who draws the feast to a close and implies criticism for the others:

> Let me request you off; our graver business
> Frowns at this levity. Gentle lords, let's part.[45]

He shows himself condemning Antony wholescale in Act III sc. vi for his excesses in declaring himself conqueror of the eastern part of the empire and apportioning different parts of Egypt and other kingdoms to Cleopatra and her sons. This is entirely against the principles of the Roman Republic. Realizing that Antony must be restrained he has already sent a message to him. It is to be noted that in sending the message he has acted on his own. He has not consulted his co-triumvir Lepidus. In other words he is already acting like an autocrat while, ironically enough, this is exactly what he accuses Antony of doing. He too is subject to the same flaw.

Added incentive is given to his warlike tendencies when Octavia, his sister and Antony's wife comes to him in the hope of bringing about a reconciliation. He tells her that she has been betrayed, that Antony has gone back to Cleopatra. This only determined him more than ever to fight Antony, though he knows what a redoubtable warrior and general he is.

We see him triumphant after Antony's disastrous defeat at Actium. He is receiving Antony's message. Antony wants to live as "a private man in Athens". It is again noticeable that he grants Cleopatra's request on condition that she forsake Antony or have him killed, but does not answer Antony's request. This again is eloquent of his astuteness as a statesman, for he knows that Antony, however humbly he might live, will still be a threat to him, but that is not the case with Cleopatra.

When he hears of the death of Antony, he is unstinted in his praise. Perhaps much of the encomium is heartfelt, but the reader can easily guess that this praise is the result of a profound sense of relief: Antony is dead and he has not had anything at all to do with this death. He frankly admits that the world is not big enough to hold both him and Antony.

When he goes to meet Cleopatra after Antony's death he treats her with great courtesy. He tells her he will always be gentle with her and even praises her on coming to know that the inventory of her property which she had given him is a false one. He himself is cunning and astute and he admires these qualities which he recognizes in her. He reassures her again and again and all the time he keeps his real intentions hidden:

> For we intend so to dispose you as
> Yourself shall give us counsel. Feed and sleep.[46]

Yet actually he means to exhibit her and her children in his triumphal progress to Rome through Syria. He has taken every precaution that she does not commit suicide as that will take away half his triumph. He, like Cleopatra, loves a show. So he would like to show Cleopatra and her children as his captives in his triumphal procession. But, being a very shrewd person, he does not tell her anything at all about it. She however, manages to make Dolabella tell her about it and cheats him of his triumph by committing suicide. However disconcerted he might be at this, he does not express his mortification before Dolabella and the others. Instead he pays tribute to her in the famous lines:

> She looks like sleep,
> As she would catch another Antony
> In her strong toil of grace.[47]

Shakespeare gives him the honour of speaking the epilogue as the establisher of moral order at the end of a tragedy, like

Fortinbras in *Hamlet*, Malcolm in *Macbeth*, Albany in *King Lear* and others in a like position. It is a dignified speech.

There have been many conjectures about his relationship with his sister Octavia. Plutarch says that he loved her very much and modern critics have naturally put the worst Freudian construction upon it. A.C. Bradley's summing up of his character is an eminently reasonable one:

> Though the character of Octavius is neither attractive nor wholly clear, his figure is invested with a certain tragic dignity because he is felt to be the Man of Destiny.[48]

The characters these as well as the minor ones (to be discussed in the next chapter) may not be morally praiseworthy, they may be the cause of ruin to themselves and to others, they may be full of complexity and thus difficult to classify, but it can never be denied that they are all eminently human. This has been pointed out by all the critics from his own days onwards. Bullough puts it very succinctly. He dicusses them one by one as described by the earlier writers like Plutarch, Cinthio et al. and then says that as far as the dramatist himself is concerned:

> What binds together the several sides of these characters is the sense of true life which they give us, the immense vitality that burns in them, through their action and their own words.[49]

REFERENCES

1. Kinsley, J., ed., *The Poems and Fables of John Dryden,* Oxford University Press, 1970 , p. 142.
2. Quoted by Fluchère, *op. cit.*, p. 131.
3. *Ibid.*, p. 136.
4. Butcher, S.H., *Aristotle's Theory of Poetry and Fine Arts.* New Delhi, Kalyani Pubs., 1981, p. 53.
5. Bullough, G., *Narrative and Dramatic Sources of Shakespeare*, Vol. V, London, Routledge and Kegan Paul, 1966, p. 57.
6. Butcher, *op. cit.*, p. 53.
7. Bradbrook, M.C., *The Growth and Structure of Elizabethan Comedy,* London, Chatto and Windus, 1955, p. 80.

8. Kronenberger, Louis, ed. *Alexander Pope: Selected Works,* New York, The Modern Library, 1951, p. 353.
9. Butcher, S.H., *op. cit.,* p. 45.
10. *Ibid.,* p. 57.
11. Stewart, J.I.M., *Character and Motive in Julius Caesar* in Ure, *op. cit.,* p. 113.
12. Dorch, T.S., transl., *Classical Literary Criticism,* Penguin Books, 1975 rpt., p. 83.
13. Scheling, F.E., *English Drama,* Pub. in 1914 by E.P. Dutt on & Co., Rept. New Delhi, S. Chand & Co., 1963, p. 135.
14. Schlegel, A.W. *op. cit.,* p. 28.
15. Act I, sc. i., lines 15-17.
16. I : ii : 125-26 ; I : ii : 137-39.
17. II : iii : 38-40.
18. II : ix : 69-71.
19. IV : xii : 99-101.
20. IV : xii : 18-21.
21. V : ii : 79-88.
22. I : i : 6-8.
23. III : vii : 40-48.
24. III : viii : 27-33.
25. IV : xiii : 24-26.
26. IV : xviii : 14-15.
27. Butcher, *op. cit.,* p. 55.
28. Dowden, *op. cit.,* p. 40.
29. Hazlitt, *op. cit.,* pp. 30-31.
30. *Op. cit.,* p. 80.
31. II : ii : 243-45.
32. Schlegel, *op. cit.,* p. 28.
33. I : iii : 64-65.
34. II : v : 61-73.
35. III : iii : 13-34.
36. *Op. cit.,* p. 66.
37. V : ii : 282-84.
38. V : ii : 348-49.
39. *Op. cit.,* pp. 42-43.
40. *Op. cit.,* p. 71.
41. *Ibid.*

42. I : iv: 16-40.
43. I : iv : 56-61.
44. II : ii : 156-58.
45. II : vii : 127-29.
46. V : ii : 185-87.
47. V : ii : 327-49.
48. *Op. cit.*, p. 72.
49. Bullough, *op. cit.*, p. 251.

7

The Minor Characters

As has been already mentioned in the last Chapter, our dramatist did not neglect his minor characters. The other dramatists of his time created a few characters of titanic stature but the others remained rather shadowy figures. Marlowe is the best example of such a dramatist. This is not the case with Shakespeare for even his minor characters have a life of their own. Not only do they provide the relevant social background but also take the action forward. The play under discussion being a historical play there are many of them. This is one of the difficulties of writing historical plays, that the canvas has to be, of necessity, a crowded one, as pointed out by A.W. Schlegel:

> In this consists the greatest difficulty of the historical dramatist : it must be a crowded extract.[1]

The canvas is a crowded one indeed in *AC*. There are 36 characters in the list of the *Dramatis Personae*, 32 of whom are named, and three more not named. Besides them there is a horde of messengers, soldiers, attendants. Out of this entire crowd only three have been treated as major characters in the last chapter. The rest of the others, it follows are minor ones. Only a few of them are going to be discussed below. In discussing them the order in which they appear in the *Dramatis Personae* will be followed.

(A) LEPIDUS

Lepidus is the first of the minor characters in *Dramatis Personae*. He is one of the triumvirs and the least important of them. Indeed, the weakness of his position had been given quite clearly in *Julius Caesar*. After having appointed him as a triumvir Antony had spoken most contemptuously of him to Octavius:

> This is a slight unmeritable man,
> Meet to be sent on errands : is it fit
> The three-fold world divided, he should stand
> One of the three to share it?[2]

He says, moreover, that they will make use of him so long as he serves their purpose and after that get rid of him. Later he is accused of treachery and divested of his portion of the kingdom. This event occurs in this play, but it is not shown. It is only mentioned in a dialogue between Enobarbus and Eros.

In this play he is seen for the first time in Act I sc. iv along with Octavius Caesar. The latter is very critical of Antony and it goes to Lepidus's credit that he stands up for Antony:

> His faults in him seem as the spots of heaven,
> More fiery by night's blackness, hereditary
> Rather than purchas'd; which he cannot change
> Then what he chooses.[3]

The important meeting of the triumvirs in which Antony's marriage with Octavia is proposed takes place in his house, so he is present throughout this scene. It has to be noted that he is eager that there should not be any quarrel between Antony and Octavius and to that end tells Enobarbus to persuade Antony to be courteous and gentle. When these two enter the stage his first attempt is to prevent any friction between them:

> That which combin'd us was most great and let not
> A leaner action rend us. What's amiss,
> May it be gently heard.[4]

His attempts as a peace-maker are effective in the beginning, for though Antony and Octavius accuse each other of different things, it is not so bad as an open quarrel. After this he keeps quiet, only interjecting here and there in order to keep things quiet and peaceful.

He appears in three scenes after this but makes no important contribution to the conversation. He is next heard of in Act

III, sc. v. in which Enobarbus and Eros exchange news. In it we come to know that in spite of the treaty signed with Pompey Octavius and he had attacked Pompey. It is during this talk that we are told how unjustly and treacherously Octavius has treated him:

> Caesar, having made use of him in the wars 'gainst Pompey, presently denied him rivality, would not let him partake in the glory of the action; and not resting here, accused him of letters he had formerly wrote to Pompey; upon his own appeal, seizes him: so the poor third is up, till death enlarge his confine.[5]

And this is the end of Lepidus in the play. He is not even talked about later, except for a few cursory references. He is not a character to leave any lasting impression on the mind of the reader.

(B) SEXTUS POMPEIUS

This Pompeius or Pompey was the son of Pompey the Great, Julius Caesar's predecessor as a conqueror. He was a warlike person and tried to get back the empire conquered by his father and taken away first by Julius Caesar and later the triumvirs. It was because he attacked the Roman Empire that Octavius had sent message to Antony to call him to Rome. The news is brought to Octavius in Act I, sc. iv and in Act II, sc. i he is shown planning his strategies with Menecrates and Menas. The messenger in sc. iv of Act I had described both of these latter as "famous pirates", but in the *Dramatis Personae* they have been designated as "Friends to Pompey" and that is how they have been shown in this scene. Pompey gives evidence of being a shrewd statesman as well as general. His evaluation of each of the triumvirs is apt:

> Mark Antony
> In Egypt sits at dinner and will make
> No wars without door; Caesar gets money where
> He loses hearts; Lepidus flatters both,
> Of both is flattered; but he neither loves
> Nor either cares for him.[6]

The only one for whom he has any respect as a warrior is Antony. He is alarmed when Varrius brings the news that Antony might arrive at Rome at any moment:

His soldiership
Is twice the other twain.[7]

Though Menas tells him that Caesar and Antony are against each other, he strewdly guesses that they will unite when threatened by him. Throughout the scene he is presented as a cool-headed and shrewd man who is capable of evaluating a situation as well as a man's nature.

In the parley scene Pompey acquits himself with dignity and acumen as indeed do the triumvirs also. He reminds them of Julius Caesar's assassination and the battle at Philippi. Then he tells them frankly that he accepts the terms offered by them and that he had come to the meeting prepared to accept them. It is he who wants the agreement to be written down and sealed with their signatures. Then a feast is agreed upon and it is he who invites them to his galley to enjoy the feast. The meeting is thus a friendly one on both sides, his as well as theirs.

Then comes the banquet scene. It is on his galley and throws new light upon his nature. He is a jovial host, generous and friendly. This is but to be expected. The new aspect of his character is revealed in his secret dialogue with Menas, who takes him aside and advises him:

Men : Wilt thou be lord of the whole world?

... ...

These three world-sharers, these competitors
Are in thy vessel: let me cut the cable;
And when we are put off, fall to their throats:
All there is thine.[8]

All is fair in love and war, and this advice might be regarded as good advice by some. Indeed Pompey does regard it as such. But any man of honour and integrity will reject it out of hand, and with scorn. Pompey too does reject it, but not with scorn. This is because he is not just a good general, but a man of honour. He is the son of Pompey the Great and cannot shame his father by acting in a dishonourable manner. All this is implied in the reply he gives. One has to understand that the three triumvirs are his guests and killing them will be against all rules of hospitality, a shameful act. It will be forever remembered by posterity as such. But he knows that it is good advice from a military point of view and wishes that it had been done without his being aware of it. He cannot give permission to do it now that he has been asked, for that will implicate him:

> Ah, this thou shouldst have done
> And not have spoke on't. In me 'tis villainy;
> In thee't had been good service.[9]

It is to be noted that his reply befits a man of honour as well as a good army-chief. He recognizes the dishonourable part of the advice as well as its practical advantages, but cannot do it.

After this he vanishes from the play. Caesar and Lepidus do not honour the treaty and attack him later on and kill him. But all that is recounted later on by Eros. He himself is not seen any more, but he leaves the impression of a noble heart and a shrewd soldier and statesman.

(C) DOMISTIUS ENOBARBUS

Enobarbus is definitely the most important of the minor characters. He is present in thirteen of the scenes and after his death only six scenes remain. He is one of the constant companions of Antony and accompanies him to Rome. He is not only a realistic figure but is eminently a realist himself. Bradley calls him a "caustic humourist" and points out that he has been almost entirely created by Shakespeare:

> The character of Enobarbus is
> practically an invention of Shakespeare's[10]

In other words, Enobarbus has been mentioned by Plutarch and others, as is but to be expected, but it is Shakespeare who has given hum a recognizable personality, a highly individual one. He has been put in the group of chorus characters by many critics but he is too much of an individual to be just a chorus character. He can, if such a classification is to be followed, be called the leader of the chorus: a person who comments upon and advises the protagonist. Indeed, besides the important persons in the play like Octavius, Lepidus and a few others, he is the only one of the followers of Antony who dares criticize and advise him and pass derogatory remarks on him as well as the others. He looks at the pomp and luxury of Rome and Cleopatra's court with a detached and humorous look that sets him apart from all others. There are persons enough to criticize Antony and Cleopatra but he is the only one who loves them and yet preserves his humorous and realistic detachment—no small feat.

He makes his entrance in the second scene of the first Act, busily supervising the laying of a banquet. It is in the last part of the scene that he comes into prominence. It is to be noticed that it is he whom Antony calls and consults about going to Rome, talking to him as to an equal. His "caustic humour" is quite apparent in this scene. Upon being told that Antony is to go to Rome he at once, most humorously, points out that:

> Cleopatra, catching the least noise of this, dies instantly; I have seen her die twenty times upon far poorer moment. I do think there is mettle in death which commits some loving act upon her, she hath such a celerity in dying.[11]

He gives these light-hearted answers to Antony, but when Antony talks seriously of the political situation and gives him some instructions, that in itself tells us that he is an astute courtier who understands international politics and does his work quickly and efficiently. He is to arrange for their departure for Rome which is a complicated affair, but all he says is a curt "I shall do it" and this brevity is eloquent of his efficiency.

He goes to Rome with Antony. It is significant that Lepidus, a triumvir himself, asks him to talk to Antony, knowing that not only does Antony pay heed to his advice, but also that he will give good advice. Then when Caesar and Antony are quarrelling he interjects from time to time trying to cool them down. Then of course, things do cool down with the proposal of marriage and after this there is the dialogue with the Romans in which the famous description of Cleopatra and her barge occurs. This speech is of nearly fifty lines, broken by enthusiastic interjections by Mecaenus and Agrippa who are listening to him goggle-eyed. Every line of this speech has been extensively commented upon and the pastiche by T.S. Eliot in *The Waste Land* has become equally famous. The picture presented is one of grandeur as well as of lasciviousness and extravagance and, as has been observed, Cleopatra becomes a "carnival figure". But more than the sumptuousness of Cleopatra it is the external and everlasting fascination she exercises that gains prominence. Mecaenus, referring to his impending marriage says that Antony will have to leave her now. The answer is a firm "no" which is not only far-sighted but full of insight into the nature of the two.

> Never; he will not:
> Age cannot wither her, nor custom stale
> Her infinite variety; other women cloy
> The appetite they feed on, but she makes hungry
> Where most she satisfies.[12]

It might be objected by critics who are very particular about character portrayal that Enobarbus is a hard-headed practical soldier and as such it is rather unlikely for him to be using such hyperbolical language. It is necessary to know that the description is not hyperbolical in the least bit. She and her appurtenances had been described in graphic detail and rich language by the writers of the books the dramatist had used for his sources. To take just One example Enobarbus says about the oars of the barge:

> The oars were silver,
> Which to the tune of flute kept stroke and made
> The water which they beat to follow faster.[13]

This might seem to be excessively, almost unrealistically grand to posterity, but preceding descriptions are even richer. Count Giulio Landi in his *Life of Cleopatra* writes thus about the oars:

> They were fashioned with such wonderful and that when they struck the water they gave out a musical sound, various and sweeter than flutes or other such instruments.[14]

This is a factual description, yet in comparison with this Enobarbus's description seems realistic and prosaic, for he says that the oars beat to music, not that they produced music themselves.

In the scene aboard Pompey's galley again, where everything is informal, we see his humour when he points at the drunk Lepidus being carried out by his servants:

> *Eno.*: There's a strong fellow, Menas (Pointing to the attendant who carries off Lepidus)
>
> *Men.*: Why?
>
> *Eno.*: He bears the third part of the world, man; see'st not?[15]

It has already been pointed out that he is the only one of Antony's followers who dares offer him good advice though he might not like it. He is a follower, but not a flatterer. One sees two examples of this in Act III, sc. vii which opens with Cleopatra threatening him with dire consequences because he had advised Antony against taking Cleopatra to Actium. She has come all the same, disregarding his advice and now threatens him. He justifies himself:

> Your presence needs must puzzle Antony;
> Take from his heart; take from his brain, from 's time,
> What should not then be spar'd.[16]

As it turns out, he had been perfectly right in advising against Cleopatra accompanying Antony for, at a crucial point in the fight she runs away with her navy and Antony follows her, thus courting defeat. Again in this same scene he advises him against fighting in the sea as his navy is weak:

> Your ships are not well mann'd;
> Your mariners are muleters, reapers, people
> Ingross'd by swift impress; ...
>
> ... ...

> Most worthy sir, you therein throw away
> The absolute soldiership you have by land.[17]

This advice too is disregarded. He is a veteran soldier and had Antony paid heed to him he would not have been defeated and perhaps history would have been written in a different manner. Later in sc. xi it is to him that Cleopatra turns for advice and he speaks fearlessly and frankly to her, not at all like a sycophant:

> What though you fled
> From that great face of war....
> .... Why should he follow?
> The itch of his affection should not then
> Have nick'd his captainship.[18]

It is in this same scene that the question of betrayal first comes into his head. Antony sends a foolhardy challenge for single combat to Caesar that Enobarbus is sure Caesar will not bother to accept or even to answer. He starts having doubts about supporting Antony any longer:

> The loyalty well held to fools does make
> Our faith mere folly.[19]

His downfall starts from here. He is still in two minds, but by the end of the scene he has decided: "I will seek/ Some way to leave him." But he still remains with him for a few more scenes.

The news of his defection is given to Antony in scene five. He responds in a manner that is as noble as can be expected of him. He sends all Enobarbus's treasures to him, with a gentle letter. Moreover, he blames himself, not Enobarbus, for this betrayal.

Enobarbus, though he has acted like a crass opportunist in deserting Antony in his hour of need is yet a man of integrity and no sooner has he left Antony than he starts regretting it:

> I have done ill,
> Of which I do accuse myself so sorely
> That I will joy no more.[20]

So much so is he full of self-blame that when he hears that Antony has sent his treasures to him he does not accept them and gives them away to the soldier who brings him the news. He has no interest in living. He wants to die, and that in as in glorious a manner as possible. He has lost all self-respect and feels guilty and wretched.

Two scenes after this, in sc. ix he dies. His death, or the manner of it, has been much talked about. He goes out at night outside Caesar's camp. It is not that he commits suicide, but, as he himself says, dies of intense self-blame and repentance at his shameful betrayal of Antony:

> ...throw my heart
> Against the flint and hardness of my fault,
> Which, being dried with grief, will break to powder
> ... ...
> But let the world rank me to register
> A master-leaver and a fugitive
> O Antony! O Antony! (Dies)[21]

It is a moving and tragic death, but does not attract much attention and gets overlooked in the turmoil of the greater tragic end of the play—the death of the hero and the heroine. But the fact cannot be denied that it is a very moving one all the more touching in that in his mind if not in action, he remains loyal to Antony. Middleton Murry has compared his death with that of Judas:

> Is it not, imagination asks, the story of Judas, told as it might have been told had a Shakespeare been there to tell it?[22]

It is paradoxical that this end wins back our sympathy for him and our mind finds nobility in him. Murry has put it very eloquently:

> Enobarbus lives in our memory not as "the master-leaver and the fugitive".... His loyalty is final and secure.[23]

(D) EROS

Eros is one of those followers of Antony who remain faithful unto death. As a matter of fact he can be said to be the most faithful of all as it is he who was with Antony in the scene in which the latter tries to commit suicide, but not before Eros has killed himself. It was on Eros that he had depended for an honourable death and from this the depth of his love and loyalty may be judged. It is this that sets him apart from other minor characters. It had been agreed between him and Antony that he will kill Antony if that was what was needed. Unable to do this, he kills himself. Such loyalty is unparalleled.

He appears in the earlier scenes of the play too, mainly as a chorus character. The most important of these scenes is the one in which occurs the exchange of news between him and Enobarbus in Act III, sc. v. It is he who tells Enobarbus how Caesar and Lepidus have gone against the treaty signed with Pompey and declared war against him and how later Caesar had betrayed Lepidus and deposed him. This scene is useful only for the news it conveys to the audience.

His next significant appearance is in Act IV, sc. xii though he comes in a few scenes before this. This scene is a very important one for him as well as for the play, for this is the one which contains Antony's attempted suicide and his own death. He and Antony enter the stage and Antony is talking to him as a friend and an equal. After he has received the false news of Cleopatra's suicide he reminds Eros of the promise he had given to Antony that if and when necessary Antony will ask him to put him to death. That is what Antony does now:

> ...On my command,
> Thou then wouldst kill me: do't; the time is come[24]

Eros is thunderstruck. He cannot bring himself to kill Antony. Instead he kills himself:

> My dear master,
> My captain and my emperor, let me say,
> Before I strike this bloody stroke, farewell.
>
> ... ...
>
> Why, there then: thus do I escape the sorrow
> Of Antony's death (kills himself).[25]

Antony speaks the appropriate epitaph on so loyal a friend and follower:

> Thrice nobler than myself!
> Thou teachest me, O valiant Eros, what
> I should and thou couldst not.[26]

Eros thus dies the death of an honest Roman, an honest friend and an honest soldier.

(E) PHILO

Philo's name comes last in the *Dramatis Personae* but in the play itself he has the honour of speaking the very first lines. He is a "Chorus" character and represents the opinion of the army as well as of Rome in general. The first 13 lines of the play, concerned with Antony and highly derogatory, are spoken by him ending with the famous lines:

> ...you shall see in him
> The triple pillar of the world transform'd
> Into a strumpet's fool; Behold and see[27]

He calls Cleopatra a gipsy and a strumpet in this one speech. He does not play any part in the play after this. It is chiefly because of this speech that he has gained notice. This is all the more significant because these thirteen lines make up the prologue.

(F) AGRIPPA

Agrippa is one of the friends of Octavius and is chiefly remarkable for the excellent advice he gives to Octavius in Act II, sc. ii. He does not speak till the scene is half over. When he sees that the talk between Antony and Octavius has reached an impasse then only does he speak and he speaks to very good purpose:

> Thou hast a sister by the mother's side,
> Admir'd Octavia...
> To hold you in perpetual amity,
> To make you brothers and to knit your hearts
> with an unslipped knot, take Antony
> Octavia to his wife.[28]

Needless to say this excellent advice at once appeals to everyone and at once an amicable agreement is reached. It is not that happy state of things as anticipated by everyone is going to be an enduring one, for soon enough Antony will be going back to Cleopatra and war will be waged between the two characters who will become brothers by marriage. The fact however that Agrippa gives very good advice and makes significant contribution to the action has to be kept in mind.

(G) SOOTHSAYER

The Soothsayer makes two significant appearances in the play, once in Act I, sc. ii and then at Rome in Act II, sc. iii. He is important because he provides the element of the supernatural in the play. As a matter of fact the supernatural manifests itself in two ways in this play, once in the guise of unearthly music heard by the soldiers before the battle and secondly through the utterances of this Soothsayer. His appearance in the earlier scene is more amusing than serious. It is to be noticed that what he says in that scene will turn out to be true, but those who hear him in that scene do not really understand. He makes five prophecies to Charmian the important ones of which are as follows:

1. You shall be more beloving than belov'd
2. You shall outlive the lady whom you serve
3. You have seen a fairer former fortune
   Than that which is to appear.[29]

Since we know that each of these is true, he gains our faith and so when he appears next we believe in him. Thus in Act II sc. iii he comes and warns Antony against Octavius:

> O Antony! stay not by his side
> ... ...
> Of that natural luck
> He beats thee 'gainst the odds; thy lustre thickens
> When he shines by. I say again, thy spirit
> Is all afraid to govern thee near him,
> But he away, 'tis noble.[30]

The supernatural element is an important feature of Elizabethan plays (*vide* Chap. 8 *infra*) and the Soothsayer is the only character who provides it in the play. So he has a special significance in it.

(H) THE CLOWN

The Clown, it should be mentioned at the outset, is not the kind of clown that kings and lords usually have. He is just a villager who provides comic relief in the play, no courtly jester.

He comes only in the last scene and speaks only 30 lines in prose yet he is as important a character as the famous Porter in *Macbeth*. This is because he carries out the same function as the Porter does and as many other like characters do in tragedies: providing comic relief (*vide* Chap. 8 *infra*).

His appearance in the play is unexpected and yet not unexpected, because a little earlier in the scene Cleopatra had whispered something to Charmian which at that time the audience may not have attached much importance to but when the Clown enters one understands at once what it was that Cleopatra had whispered to Charmian. The Clown has brought her the asps or vipers with which she will be able to commit suicide. Thus she will be able to escape the indignity of being exhibited in Caesar's triumphal procession as his captive. She asks him:

> Hast thou the pretty worm of Nilus there
>
> That kills and pains not?
>
> *Clo.*: Truly, I have him, but I would not be party that should desire you to touch him for his biting is immortal; those that do die of't do seldom or never recover.[31]

It is significant that he uses the word "immortal" which Cleopatra will use as soon as he goes out. The dialogue between the two of them go on for a few more lines. He is a simple fellow and speaks simply, with comic overtones. Twice does he wish her "joy of the worm."

This appearance of the Clown at such a moment has been much commented upon. A.C. Bradley's comment may be quoted here. While writing on the use of "humour" or "semi-humorous passages" in the play he observes:

> ...their occasional introduction in the fourth Act or even later affords variety and relief and also heightens by contrast the tragic feeling.[32]

Then, after citing instances from other plays he comes to the play under discussion and even today, more than a century later, his remark remains relevant and eminently quotable. This, in spite of there having been important observations by many later critics:

> But the acme of audacity is reached in *Antony and Cleopatra* when, quite close to the end, the old countryman who brings the asps discourses to Cleopatra on the virtues and vices of the worm.[33]

(I) THE MESSENGER

The Soothsayer and the Clown are not what are called "named characters" for they do not have names though their designation is given. The many messengers too are like them. Those whose functions are given though not their names can also be called named characters though strictly speaking they should not. One of the messengers, however, deserves special mention. He is the one who brings Cleopatra the news of Antony's marriages to Octavia (Act II, sc. iv) and then again reappears in Act III, sc. iii to give her a description of Octavia's personality. Not only is he an individual of some interest in himself, he gains importance because of the way in which he reveals aspects of Cleopatra's character not seen elsewhere.

In the first of his two appearances he is a simple and conscientious Messenger whose duty it is to give a realistic picture and a true message. But Cleopatra's reaction on hearing the truth is totally unexpected. She turns into a virago in the twinkling of an eye, abuses him, beats him, pulls him up and down by the hair and finally takes a dagger to kill him Granville-Barker describes her as:

> ...most unlike the golden vision on Cydnus, a spitting fury that hales the messenger of Antony's faithlessness up and down by the hairs of his head.[34]

The Messenger is dutiful, he will give her the truth, though that might put him in danger of his life. In this scene he brings to the surface a hitherto unknown aspect of Cleopatra's nature.

In his next appearance it can be seen that he has learnt his lesson, though at the cost of truthfulness. He is now saying whatever will please Cleopatra, not that which is true. We have to admire this exhibition of common sense in him. It helps him to survive. Cleopatra had sent him to find out the kind of person Octavia was. He feels his way carefully when talking to her and answers her questions the way she would like. He reports Octavia to be short, low-voiced, clumsy in her movements, a widow of 30 years, round in face, with brown hair and a low forehead (*vide* Chap. 6, sec. 'd. *supra*). All this is just what she wants to hear and this time, instead of being abused and threatened, he get praised and gets gold and on top of that on apology from Cleopatra for her former roughness. A most politic fellow, to describe him in Elizabethan language.

In this dialogue Cleopatra shows herself to be an extremely gullible woman. She hears what she wants to hear and believes all that implicitly. It does not cross her mind that he might be lying to her. What is surprising is that she belongs to a dynasty of rulers and should know that the truth is hardly ever told to a powerful man. She did not want to believe the first message he had brought, but now she believes all that he tells her. Perhaps it is because he had been truthful in the former instance, but all the same the Messenger says Octavia is quite an unattractive person. Shakespeare has endowed this particular Messenger with great individuality.

(J) OCTAVIA

Octavia is the only minor female character in the play for the other two, Iras and Charmian, are attendants: She appears four times in the play and is presented as a quiet and dignified character, the very opposite of Cleopatra. In fact she is not even a good and effective foil to her.

It becomes quite clear from her first appearance that she is determined to be a good wife and a good sister. She knows that her marriage is of great political significance. In this scene (Act II, sc. iii) she speaks about two lines and in her second appearance, when she bids farewell to her brother also speaks about two lines only. In her next appearance, which is at Athens we see her and Antony alone for the first time. In this scene she takes a proper part in the dialogue.

Antony has just received the news that Octavius has not honoured the treaty with Pompey and has declared war upon him. He has also decried Antony publicly. Octavia tries to pacify him. She is in a most unenviable position, for on one hand there is her brother and on the other her husband, for whom then, can she or should she, pray?

> A more unhappy lady,
> If this division chance, ne'er stood between,
> Praying for both parts.[35]

Antony, in a praiseworthy and magnanimous manner, allows her to go to Rome as a peace-maker, and tells her to take whatever and whoever she wants to be with her on her journey. She is most anxious to effect a reconciliation:

> The love of power make me weak, most weak,
> Your reconciler! Wars 'twixt you twain would be
> As if the world should cleave.[36]

We see her next, with just one intervening link-scene in between, in Rome. Octavius Caesar has been conferring with Agrippa about what to do with Antony, who has acted very much against the principles of the Roman Republic when she appears. She is most cordially welcomed by him and has hardly started to speak when Caesar tells her that Antony has betrayed her. She had left him in Athens and she thinks him to be still there, patiently awaiting her return. He opens her eyes, very gently:

> No, my most wrong'd sister; Cleopatra
> Hath nodded him to her. He hath given his empire
> Up to a whore.[37]

Octavia, deeply offended, has no difficulty in believing him. But it is noticeable that in her brief speech after this she does not blame Antony or accuse him with adultery though the others do. Instead she blames her fate:

> Ay me, most wretched,
> That have my heart parted betwixt two friends
> That do afflict each other.[38]

After this we do not see her gain. She is quiet and dignified; a more glaring contrast to Cleopatra can hardly be found. She is no match for Cleopatra. For that matter, no one is.

(K) IRAS AND CHARMIAN

These two attendants of Cleopatra are always together. They are not just faithful to her, they love her very deeply. It is no ordinary love but an intense adoration that is literally faithful even unto death. They are happy when she is happy and sad when she is so. This is not because of any sycophancy but is the result of genuine love. Throughout the play they never criticise her, even in an aside. They sympathise with her so intensely that Charmian helps her to commit suicide by arranging for the Clown to bring asps. Iras kisses her farewell and dies then and there, without any help from the asps. It is left for Charmian to speak what are, after Enobarbus's speech, the best-known lines about Cleopatra. She arranges the dead body with infinite tenderness in a manner that is becoming:

> Now boast thee, death, in thy possession lies
> A lass unparallel'd. Downy windows, close;
> A golden Phoebus never be beheld
> Of eyes again so royal.[39]

After having arranged Cleopatra's crown which was sitting askew on her head, she takes one of the asps and thus commits suicide.

It speaks volumes for Cleopatra as a woman that she had won the love of these two to such an extent that they choose to die with her rather than live without her. It is one of the best things that can be said about her, for it proves her human qualities.

REFERENCES

1. Schlegel, A.W. in Brown J.R. *op. cit.*, p. 27.
2. *Julius Caesar*, Act IV: sc. i: lines 12-15.
3. AC, I : iv : 12-15.
4. II : it : 18-20.
5. III : v : 7-13.
6. II : i : 11-16.
7. II : i : 34-35.
8. II : vii : 69-80.
9. II : vii : 80-82.

10. Bradley, A.C., in Brown, J.R., *op.cit.*, p. 84.
11. I : ii : 149-54.
12. II : ii : 242-45.
13. II : ii : 202-04.
14. Bullough, G., *op. cit.*, p. 352.
15. II : vii : 95-97.
16. III : vii : 10-12.
17. III : vii : 34-42.
18. III : xi : 4-8.
19. III : xi : 42-43.
20. IV : vi : 18-20.
21. IV : ix : 15-23.
22. Murry, J.M. in Brown, *op. cit.,* p. 118.
23. *Ibid.*
24. IV : xii : 66-67.
25. IV : xii : 89-95.
26. IV : xii : 95-97.
27. I : i : 11-13.
28. I : ii : 124-34.
29. I ; ii : 24-36.
30. II : iii : 18-30.
31. V : ii : 242-47.
32. *op. cit.* p. 47.
33. *Ibid.*
34. Granville-Barker, *The Play's Construction*, in Brown, J.R., *op. cit.,* p. 89.
35. III. iv : 12-14.
36. III : iii : 29-32.
37. III : vi : 65-67.
38. III : vi : 76-78.
39. V : ii : 317-20.

8

The Plot Structure

Elizabethan dramatists, specially the university wits, had been deeply influenced by classical drama and the technique followed in it. But Shakespeare was not a poet to be bound down by any rules or conventions. He was a creator and, as such, followed his own rules. This is not to say that he did not follow any rules at all. Most certainly he did, but not always. There are many classical rules he did not follow. Usually however, he followed the stage conventions of his own time, as will be seen in this chapter later. The neo-classical dramatists and critics have many complaints against his drama and as has been proved again and again he had proved to be eminently successful without bothering to follow a careful plot methodically. Harley Granville-Barker has pointed out:

> We should never, probably, think of Shakespeare as sitting down to construct a play as an architect must design a house.[1]

(A) THE CLASSICAL RULES AND AC

In order to know anything at all about classical rules it is necessary to know Aristotle's definition of tragedy:

> Tragedy, then, is the imitation of an action that is serious, complete and of a given magnitude; in language embellished with each kind of artistic ornament, the several kinds being found in separate parts of the play; in the form of action, not of narration; through pity and fear effecting the proper purgation of these emotions.[2]

This definition is full of many complex implications that have been expounded and commented upon by scholars. The Elizabethans treated it as a point of reference. It is the root from which the rules that shall now be mentioned have originated.

The rules of the unities are the best-known of all the rules. There are three of these rules: (a) the unity of Action, (b) the unity of Time and (c) the unity of Place. It is a well-known fact that our poet did not take these rules very seriously, and, except for *The Tempest*, did not observe them carefully. Hazlitt has remarked in this connection that over-attention to the unities can be harmful to a play:

> The jealous attention which has been paid to the unities, both of time and place has taken away the principle of perspective in the drama.[3]

(a) The Unity of Action

This is the most important of the three unities and refers directly to the definition given above. Aristotle points out that the action of a tragedy is "serious". In other words, there should not be any mingling of trivial action with the serious. This rule is specially relevant for tragedies (though it is applied to comedies as well) for pity and terror, which are the emotions peculiar to tragedies are emotions roused by serious action. Shakespeare does not observe this rule (nor do many of the other dramatists of his time) for in his tragedies there are frequent comic scenes. There are quite a few such scenes in *AC* as well, which will be studied more in detail later.

(b) The Unity of Time

Aristotle gives a full day, "a single revolution of the sun" for the completion of the action of a play. This rule is quite difficult to follow, but it should be known that this and all the other classical rules had been most carefully observed by Ben Jonson. Shakespeare himself has observed it in *The Tempest.*

It is, however, not possible to observe this rule in the Chronicle plays or the other historical plays. Now *AC* is a historical tragedy and naturally enough a long span of time has been covered in it. Shakespeare has concentrated nearly ten years of history into about two years, since the play starts in 40 B.C. some little time after Antony and Cleopatra have met, and ends with their deaths in 30 B.C. Yet the miraculous thing is that there is never any sense of any awkwardness as far as the time factor is concerned. It will be short-sighted to expect unity of time in such a play, or to condemn it for violation of this rule. Shakespeare however has presented the action, scene by scene, in so continuous a manner that there is no difficulty in following the story. The reader is not made aware of the fact that any long or appreciable length of time has passed between one scene and another.

This sense of continuity was helped for the spectator of his own time by the fact that the play, originally, had no act or scene divisions at all. Such divisions introduce pauses in the performance and these pauses easily indicate the passing of time and many other changes as well. Elizabethan plays, as a rule, did not have act or scene divisions. These were marked out by the stage-manager according to the action in the play. He would introduce a break if and when such a break was dramatically indicated. But in the case of *AC*, Granville-Barker has firmly asserted:

> Now, whatever other dramatists may have done in other plays, which may have been the custom of the public and private theatres for which he wrote...in this play there is no dramatically indicated act-division at all.[4]

The events thus seem to follow each other in a quite systematic and acceptable way. One also allows for time spent in journeying from one place to another, for example Antony's journey to Rome, etc. So the flow of events, though it happened in the past during ten long years, yet is accepted as happening in dramatic time without any appreciable break. The span of time covered never became as notorious as, for example, that of *The Winter's Tale* where sixteen years pass in the middle of the play. There is no such anomaly in *AC*. Instead as another critic, following Granville-Barker, points out the plot as a series of actions flowing on in an uninterrupted manner:

> The plot is now seen to be a careful pattern of interweaving and contrasting episodes, all duly subordinated to the main design: the presentation of Antony and Cleopatra in the broad context of the Roman Empire.[5]

(c) The Unity of Place

This rule implies that all the action should take place in one place only. It should be remembered, however, that this rule was not specifically recommended by Aristotle. The critics of the Italian Renaissance, like Scaliger, Minturno and Castelvetro were responsible for this rule. The Elizabethans interpreted it to mean that there should be no changes of scenes and as such the rule was very difficult to follow. The only one who followed it was Ben Jonson and even he allows himself a lot of freedom. Shakespeare does not follow it in *AC* and most of his plays. He had been very strongly criticised for the violation of this rule by the neo-classical critics. Yet it should be kept in mind that the greatest of the neo-classical critics Dr. Johnson, does not castigate him. Instead he defends Shakespeare and this famous defence shows his own greatness as a critic. As he specifically refers to *AC* in this connection it should be read with attention. But before that it will be necessary to know, roughly, the location of the important scenes and Acts.

The scenes range from Alexandria to Rome and some are located in Pompey's ship, Syria, Athens and Actium. Even when several scenes take place in one place, like Rome, the locale changes from one house to another, etc. Roughly speaking, 13 scenes are located in Alexandria and six in Rome. The rest of the 38 scenes are scattered here and there. Space-wise, the play has great range and variety. It is with objections related to his that Dr. Johnson frames his famous defence:

> The objections arising from the impossibility of passing the first hour at Alexandria and the next at Rome suppose that when the play opens the spectator really imagines himself at Alexandria....
>
> The truth is that the spectators are always in their senses and know from the first act to the last that the

> stage is only a stage and that the players are only players.[6]

This admirable defence rests, as much of Dr. Johnson's criticism does, upon hard-headed common sense and with this defence in mind Shakespeare's frequent changes of location in *AC* become acceptable. It should also be noted that he makes most effective use of the balcony provided in Elizabethan stage in the monument scene at the end of Act IV.

Many other rules, in addition to these, had been laid down by Aristotle which were later expanded by other critics. Donatus's treatise on drama was one such work. He has explained Aristotle's theory in detail and also added his own corollaries to them. According to him the first section of the play is Prologue. This actually used to be a short speech coming before the actual action started. Marlowe's Prologue to *Dr. Faustus* is a very good example of a prologue in the strictly classical manner. Our poet too has written prologues to a few of his plays but usually he incorporates them within the first scene of the play, and this is the case with *AC*.

There are some other features that are part of the classical concept of tragedy *Peripeteia* or the Reversal of fortune is one of them. This is an indispensable part of a tragedy as it implies the fall of the hero from a high to a low status. It has been explained by Aristotle. Explaining the ideal plot for a tragedy he rejects three outlines and at the end fixes on the plot that gives a rather good man falling from prosperity into adversity. The turn of fortune in *AC* too follows the same pattern. We see Antony at first in the full flush of might and glory. Then little by little, from the second part of the play onwards, comes his downfall till, after his second defeat he comes to know about the supposed death of Cleopatra and kills himself.

Another important feature of the tragic plot is *Anagnorisis* or Recognition. This, at its crudest level, involves the mutual recognition of two characters who have been separated, as happens in *Twelfth Night* when Viola and Sebastian recognize each other. The most subtle recognition is the one which occurs when a character recognizes his own nature. It occurs quite a few times in *AC* when Antony recognizes the weakness in his own character, but these are fitful and do not herald any lasting change. No such self-recognition occurs in Cleopatra. Hers remains an entirely superficial one right till the end.

Keeping these deficiencies in mind, it should be remembered that Dr. Johnson is not the only neo-classicist who has defended Shakespeare. Pope is no less eloquent. According to him our poet should not be judged by classical Aristotelian rules at all. The appeal, as in Dr. Johnson, is once more to common sense:

> To judge therefore of Shakespeare by Aristotelian rules is like trying a man by the law of one country, who acted under those of another.[7]

(B) CERTAIN ELIZABETHAN FEATURES

As Aristotle's definition of tragedy states a tragedy should have but one action, i.e. one plot. Intrigues will be there, but a full-fledged sub-plot is against the rules. They are permitted in comedies particularly in the New Comedy, but not in tragedies. Elizabethan tragedies however, often have a sub-plot. Usually the sub-plot is a comic one and thus violates the unity of action twice over. Multiplicity of plot is a notable feature of Elizabethan plays, as also is the adoption of disguises. Both of these, however, can be omitted from this discussion as they do not occur in *AC*.

The soliloquy is an important feature of Elizabethan plays. They are speeches delivered by a character when he is alone on the stage. They deal with the speaker's thoughts. The character may tell us what he is going to do in future, he may tell us about his impression of events that have happened, etc. Soliloquies are like talking aloud. Hamlet's soliloquies are famous ones. So far as this aspect of *AC* is concerned, it is surprising that there are so few soliloquies. The hero and the heroine, for that matter, are hardly ever alone on the stage. There are a few short soliloquies by Antony. There are actually only four occasions when he is alone on the stage and the soliloquies are never of any considerable length. The longest of them (13 lines) occurs in Act IV, sc. x after Antony's final defeat. The most moving of them is part of a speech delivered when he receives the news of Cleopatra's supposed suicide. He asks Eros to take off his armour and then asks to be left alone. The speech, starting with "Unarm Eros" continues as a soliloquy:

> I will o'ertake thee, Cleopatra, and
> Weep for my pardon. So it must be, for now
> All length is torture; since the torch is out,
> Lie down, and stray no further.[8]

So there are a few soliloquies by Antony, but none from Cleopatra. She is never alone on the stage. Actually the two of them hardly ever have the chance to commune with themselves, which is actually what a soliloquy is. It is a surprising fact that though Shakespeare makes most effective use of this device in other plays there are no remarkable soliloquies in *AC* except the few mentioned above. They too are not full-fledged soliloquies, but part of a longer speech.

The element of the supernatural is another important feature of Elizabethan plays. So far as Shakespeare's plays are concerned, he has made repeated use of the supernatural, element. In a *Midsummer Night's Dream* and *The Tempest*, supernatural characters take an active part in the action. These are exceptions, but in other plays also such figures indirectly influence the action as the three witches in *Macbeth* and the Ghost in *Hamlet* do. In *AC* as in *Julius Caesar* the influence exercised by supernatural elements is even less direct, but it exists, creating an atmosphere of ominous disaster. It provides the element of the wonderful or the Marvellous that is so often present in drama. Moreover it is recognized by Aristotle:

> The element of the wonderful is required in tragedy.... The poet should prefer probable impossibilities to improbable possibilities.[9]

This element is also present in *AC*, though not in as prominent a manner as in *Hamlet* or *Macbeth*. Here it comes twice, once in the soothsayer's warning to Antony (Act II, sc. iii) and then again in the unearthly music heard by the guards.

Soothsayers and such people were very common in Elizabethan plays and the Romans too believed in them implicitly. There is a most important Soothsayer in *Julius Caesar*. Whose warning to Caesar to "beware the ides of March" has become famous. In this play the Soothsayer first comes in Act I, sc. ii where the women attending Cleopatra consult him. This is a light-hearted scene. But when he next makes his appearance in Act II, sc. iii it is a serious warning. He says Antony will never rise in the world so long as he stands near Octavius. He should go away from Rome.

> Thy demon—that's thy spirit which keeps thee,—is
> Noble, courageous, high, unmatchable,
> Where Caesar is not; but near him thy angle
> Becomes a fear, as being o'erpower'd[10]

He makes the whole thing even clearer to Antony by talking of playing at dice, or indeed any game:

> If thou dost play with him at any game
> Thou art sure to lose and, of that natural luck
> He beats thee 'gainst the odd; thy lustre thickens
> When he shines by.[11]

Antony is naturally alarmed—all the more so as he has already noticed that "the very dice obey him" that is, Octavius who wins whatever game is played.

This appearance of the supernatural is dependent on a human character—the Soothsayer. The next time the supernatural manifests itself independently of any human agent in what A.C. Bradley has called "the strangely effective scene".

This is the third scene of Act IV, on the eve of the last battle. Two soldiers are on guard duty outside the palace at Alexandria. Two more join them. All four then hear the "music of hautboys under the stage". At first they think that it is coming from the air, then they realize it is coming from under the earth. Then they wonder about what this would mean. In order to find out if the other guards have heard the music or not they move on to the next post and there also the soldiers have heard the music. The second of them offers an explanation:

> 'Tis the god Hercules, whom Antony lov'd,
> Now leaves him.[12]

No one disagrees with this interpretation, so it is reasonable to think that this is what the poet too means. This event is fully in accord with what Aristotle calls "Probable impossibilities" and "improbable possibilities". It creates an atmosphere of ominous disaster most successfully, by anticipating the tragic doom of Antony.

The Elizabethan plays are also marked by a violation of the Aristotelian unity of action. It was not only Shakespeare who violated this rule, but nearly every body else except Ben Jonson who scrupulously observed all the unities. Otherwise it is common to find two features in Elizabethan plays which are the results of the violation of this rule.

When Aristotle says that tragedy is the "imitation of an action that is serious and complete in itself" he is implying two things (a) that in a tragedy the action should be serious, that is, no comic element should be there and (b) that there should be one action, not several, that is, the play should be a single-plotted one. Incidentally, this is the only rule that Ben Jonson has not observed, for none of his plays is single-plotted. Now, nearly all Elizabethan tragedies have comic scenes in them, certainly all of Shakespeare's have. Even *Macbeth* which is the darkest of all the tragedies, has at least one speech by the Porter to give comic relief, though it is not a full scene. The extreme example of such a case is Marlow's *Dr Faustus* in which the comic scenes are equal in number to the serious ones.

As far as *AC* is concerned there are a few light-hearted scenes like the second scene of Act I in which the mood is one of merriment, with jokes by the court-women as they consult the Soothsayer. It is but part of a scene, not an independent scene by itself, but apart from this there are two occasions which are definitely comic ones, intended to produce laughter. The first of them is the long banquet scene aboard Pompey's galley. This entire scene is a comic one (Act II, sc. viii), the entire dialogue (with exception of the one between Menas and Pompey) is a comic one. All of them are drunk and Antony is having fun with the other guests, making fools of them:

Lep. : What manner of thing is your crocodile?

Ant. : It is short sir, like itself; and it is broad as it has breadth; it is just so high as it is, and moves with its own organs; it lives by that which nourisheth it; and the elements once out of it, it transmigrates.

Lep. : What colour is it of?

Ant. : Of its own colour, too.[13]

The conversation goes on in this vein. Every one is drunk. Lepidus is so drunk that he has to be carried away by his servant and Enobarbus's joke on it has already been quoted. After this there is song and dance. The scene provides innocent merry-making and laughter.

The next comic relief however is not one of innocent merry-making, it is far more serious. It is part of the last scene and has already been commended upon (*vide* Chap. 4 and Chap. 7 *supra*). It occurs when the Clown enters with the basket of asps. His words provide unintentional comic relief, for he speaks without any comic intentions, but it is sure to produce laughter in the audience:

Cleo. : Will't eat me?

Clown : You must not think I am so simple but I know the devil himself will not eat a woman; I know that a woman is a dish for the gods, if the devil dress her not.[14]

Commenting on such comic scenes A.C. Bradley, observes that such scenes usually come early in the play, as indeed the two former scenes referred to above do, but that sometimes they are introduced in Act IV or even later. He gives several instances from *Macbeth, Coriolanus* and *Hamlet*. But this clown scene in *AC* is the supreme example:

> But the acme of audacity is reached
> in *Antony and Cleopatra.*[15]

He points out that the last words of line Clown contain the word "immortal" and they are immediately followed by Cleopatra's magnificent speech beginning "Give me my robes" which has the word "immortal" in the very second line. It is extremely difficult to determine whether this clown scene truly brings comic relief or just serves to intensity dramatic suspense. Whatever the effect is thought to be by critics, the scene is a comic one.

The other Elizabethan features related to the unity of action is the use of more than one plot. Almost all Elizabethan plays have more than one plot and it is rare to come across a single-plotted play. *AC* is one such rare play. It has just one plot and many intrigues, but no sub-plot—nothing that goes on for long enough to be called one. Shakespeare has gone against contemporary convention in this matter.

It is to be seen thus that Shakespeare observed or violated classical rules according to the needs of the plot and did the same with Elizabethan conventions. Coleridge has said:

> A pedant different from a master in cramping himself with certain established rules, whereas the master regarded rules as always controllable by and subservient to the end.[16]

(C) THE SOURCES OF AC

It was the custom for Elizabethan dramatists to take the material for their plays from already existing sources, like pre-existing plays, romances, narrative poems, histories, etc. This, indeed, used to be done in classical times also. The study of Shakespeare's sources has become one of the recognized branches of literary criticism of his plays. It reveals his powers of organization as nothing else does. He selected materials from many sources, concentrating some, expanding some, rejecting some and retaining some according to his needs. Verity sums it up:

> His position is that of the Greek tragedians. He dealt with the existing material of drama...much as they dealt with the cycles of Greek traditional myth: and exercising the same sovereign liberty of appropriate, he turned it to the same account.[17]

Geoffrey Bullough has shown Shakespeare's indebtedness to Plutarch, but besides being indebted to Lord North's translation of Plutarch's famous *Lives* there were many other works which Shakespeare turned to at the time of writing this play. He classifies the sources Shakespeare used into ten kinds as follows:

1. ***Source*** : Plutarch's *Lives of the Noble Grecians and Romans*, translated by Sir Thomas North (1579). The Life of Antony.
2. ***Probable Source*** : From *The Life of Octavius Caesar Augustus* in North's *Plutarch* (1603 edn.) by S. Goulart.
3. ***Analogues***: From Lucan's *Pharsalia* transl. by Thomas May (1627). The Tenth Booke.
4. ***Translation of Analogue*** : From *The Antiquities of the Jews* by Flavius Josephus, transl. by Thomas Lodge (1602).
5. ***Analogue*** : From *The Roman Histories of Flavius* transl. by E.M.B.[olton][1619].
6. ***Source*** : From *The Civil Wars* by Appian of Alexandria, transl. by W.B. (1578).
7. ***Translation of Analogue*** : From *The Deeds of Caesar.* Anon. (13th century).
8. ***Summary of Analogue*** : *Cleopatra* by G.B. Giraldi Cinthio (1583 edn.).
9. ***Analogue*** : *The Tragedie of Antonie* by Robert Garnier, transl. by Mary Herbert (Sidney) 1595.
10. ***Probable Source*** : *The Tragedy of Cleopatra* by Samuel Daniel (1599 edn.).

For this play he has taken the *Life of Antony* as his main source out of Plutarch. But it cannot be doubted that the other books listed above existed for reference and Shakespeare turned to Plutarch for most of his information. He took the events from him as well as the characters. Inspecting the characters in the light of his creative talent, he developed them and the relationship between them. Plutarch was not a mere recorder of events, he also evaluated the characters and this where Shakespeare is most indebted to him:

> For what Shakespeare learned from Plutarch was to represent more clearly than before the paradoxes of

> human motives, the mixture of good and evil in the same person.[18]

This chapter however is more concerned with plot than with character and it is here that our poet's genius for organization comes to the fore. He altered many details for the sake of greater dramatic effect. Now let us look at the sources he used.

This is the order in which Bullough has arranged his material. It will be noticed that actually the sources fall under three headings: (a) sources, (b) probable source, and (c) analogues. This last item contains translations and a summary as well. A careful study of these works will enable the student to see how the dramatist has adjusted, compressed, selected and expanded his material to create the wonderful play of *AC*. One or two examples might be given of Shakespeare's masterly organization of his material. Here is an example of compression.

Plutarch gives that after Antony had followed the fleeing Cleopatra at the battle of Actium his soldiers continued to fight for hours and hours and later kept together for seven days, hoping for his eventual return, though in vain:

> Many plainly sawe Antonius flie, and yet could hardly believe it.... And yet his soldier still wished for him and even hoped that he would come by some means or other unto them. Furthermore, they shewed themselves so valliant and faithful unto him, that after they certainly knewe he was fled, they kept themselves whole together for seven daies.[19]

Shakespeare changes, or rather concentrates, all this to a few minutes. Thus in Act III, sc. viii all this is told in just thirty lines. Enobarbus enters exclaiming "Naught, naught, all naught!" Then Scarus tells him how Antony had followed the fleeing Cleopatra, and Canidius decides to leave him as six other kings have already done. The hours of fighting without a leader and the loyal waiting for seven days by the entire army is concentrated into Enobarbus's continued fidelity, though he too has his doubts:

> I'll yet follow
> The wounded chance of Antony, though my reason
> Sits in the wind against me.[20]

An example of transposition of an event to make it even more effective occurs in Enobarbus's defection. In Plutarch this occurs before the disaster at Actium, but Shakespeare puts it just before the catastrophe. He follows Plutarch however, in making him die of a broken heart:

> ...and the same day as though he gave him to understand that he repented his open treason, he died immediately after.[21]

Plutarch calls him Domitius and Shakespeare calls him Domitius Enobarbus and the character is, as Bradley has pointed out, almost entirely invented by Shakespeare. What has to be remembered in this instance is that Shakespeare took a minor character from Plutarch and some of the events concerned with him and used it in his own way, making it all the more effective.

Apart from the works listed by Bullough, Shakespeare and other Elizabethans would have been familiar with many other works concerned with the story, ranging from mediaeval tales to Renaissance *exempla* to Senecan drama. Chaucer's portrait of Cleopatra in *Legand of Good Women* is the very first of the saint's lives given by him. The most prominent of the Senecan dramas, Garnier's *Marc Antoine* and Samuel Daniel's *Cleopatra* have already been cited by Bullough. All these works, if they are carefully compared with Shakespeare's will reveal his mastery, not only over the element of plot-structure but over style and character as well.

(D) THE PLOT OF AC

It has already been pointed out (*vide* Chap. 3, *supra*) that as far as the matter of the form of the play goes, A.C. Bradley placed it higher than the plays of the third phase. He points out that the plays of the fourth phase have been placed there "because of a difference in substance and spirit", but that if one takes into consideration not only the style but also the technique used in construction, then the division would be different:

> If a fourth Period were admitted on grounds of form, it ought to begin with *AC.*[22]

In other words the form or the plot-construction of *AC* is somewhat different from those of the other plays. First of all it has no sub-plots. There is just the one plot though are many intrigues. This unilinear plot makes for a tight and neatly constructed play. Not only that—there is no separate Prologue or Epilogue which makes the play even more streamlined. The first few lines of the play serve as the Prologue. Actually the lines spoken before the entrance of the hero and the heroine are treated as the Prologue by Una Ellis-Fermor:

> In *Antony and Cleopatra* the mood is given...briefly in thirteen lines which also serve as a partial prologue.[23]

The play proceeds on its way after this in a leisurely manner. As Bradley has pointed out, the first half of the play is also comparable with *Othello* in this connection. It is in the second half that the play picks up speed.

Conflict, which is an essential part of a tragedy, is present in the play under different aspects. It is introduced quite early in the play, not through actual action but through report. In the second scene the messenger tells Antony of the warfare introduced by Fulvia and Pompey and battle is the most obvious kind of conflict. But it is not presented on he stage as it will be in the second part, with events coming thick and fast. A more subtle kind of conflict, verbal quarrel between different characters is present in Act II, sc. ii in which Antony and Caesar have a dispute. Caesar accuses Antony of neglecting his duties and Antony answers him. It is not a heated quarrel, for Lepidus and Enobarbus keep on trying to quieten the two all the time, and very soon, with Agrippa's proposal, conflict vanishes and amity reigns. The parley-scene also results in the peace-treaty, though the possibility of conflict had been there in the background. Thus in this part of the play, with its implied (Antony's marriage) and the practical (the banquet aboard Pompey's galley), there are no fights and battles, or conflict of an obvious kind.

A subtle kind of conflict however, is present from the beginning. There is the mental conflict between love and duty in Antony's mind. He is deeply in love with Cleopatra yet he realizes that it is an enervating love, that he will have to break this bond, or he will be ruined:

I must from this enchanting queen break off;
Ten thousand harms more than the ills I know.
My idleness doth hatch.[24]

A little later he says to Enobarbus: "She is cunning past man's thought" and still later exclaims, "Would I had never seen her!" So the conflict between love and duty rages in his heart and later in the play it gets more and more acute.

Conflict is there in the open in the second half of the play when Octavia reaches Rome. From now on there is no possibility of any amicable settlement between Antony and Octavius Caesar. Conflict in its most obvious form, battle by sea and on land, becomes inevitable. Antony does try for reconciliation by allowing Octavia to approach Caesar, but he also prepares for war:

Yourself shall go between's : the mean time, lady,
I'll raise the preparations of a war.[25]

The battle at Actium ends ingloriously in flight. This is represented, as Granville-Barker points out, in a symbolic manner, as it cannot very well be presented on the stage:

> The first day's fighting is compressed in the symbolism (it is little else) of a dozen lines of dialogue and business.... This symbolism of the war is not in itself dramatic.[26]

However symbolic and undramatic it might be, it is still conflict in the most obvious form. Then comes the next stage of the battle in which Antony is victorious at first, then, through Cleopatra's betrayal, he is finally defeated and warfare, that is to say all conflict, comes to an end.

Mental conflict however, reaches great intensity, not once but several times, in the play. First of all there is the open conflict between Caesar and Antony and later between Antony and Cleopatra. This latter comes into prominence after her flight from the sea-battle. Antony reproaches her, though rather mildly:

Ant. : O! Whither hast thouled me, Egypt? see
How I convey my shame out of thine eyes...

Cl. : O my lord, my lord!
Forgive my fearful sails : I little thought
You would have follow'd.
Ant. : Egypt, thou knew'st too well
My heart is to thy rudder tied by the strings...
Cl. : O my pardon.
Ant. : ...Now I must
To the young man send humble treaties...
...You did know
How much you were my conqueror.[27]

Then he comes to know of Caesar's proposal to her that she will not be victimized by him if she surrenders Antony to him. He is, as is but to be expected, extremely bitter and abuses her very strongly, accusing her of having been the mistress of Pompey and Julius Caesar before meeting him. She manages to quieten him this time too, but it is clear that his faith in her has got shaken.

After the second betrayal he is far more bitter and does not even allow her to speak, far less forgive her as he did the first time:

Ah! thou spell. Avaunt!
Cl. : Why is my lord enrag'd against his love?
Ant. : Vanish or I shall give thee thy deserving.[28]

This particular conflict is out in the open but the inner conflict in his mind is far stronger. There had been conflict in his heart in the earlier scenes, conflict between love and duty. Later this conflict centres around Cleopatra. When he joins battle with Caesar he is happy, for he is doing his duty as a soldier, but almost at once, because of Cleopatra's repeated capriciousness there is a raging conflict in his heart as he loves, yet despises her. An observation of A.C. Bradley is relevant in this connection. Referring to her faithlessness he compares her with the portrayal of Cressida in *Troilus and Cressida* as well as the dark lady of the sonnets and quotes two lines:

> When my love swears she is made of truth,
> I do believe her, though I know she lies.[29]

The element of catastrophe in the play is very significant. Donatus's famous treatise mentioned earlier gives Act V to this element. But there is a little difficulty as far as *AC* is concerned. Here Antony's death takes place in Act IV and Cleopatra's at the end of Act V, so the catastrophe is a very prolonged one. Discussing this particular feature of Shakespearean tragedy, Bradley points out that the catastrophe is extended in other plays also, and observes that an extended catastrophe is made possible only when there is another character besides the hero, who is equally important. This is what happens in *Othello* in which there is a gap of considerable time between the death of Desdemona and that of Othello. Likewise in *Macbeth* the catastrophe is extended to cover the death of Lady Macbeth and then of Macbeth. In both of these cases the catastrophe is spread over the entire fifth Act. But *AC* is extraordinary in that here it is spread over not one, but two acts. Antony dies after line no. 62 "No better than a style? O! see my women", is spoken by Cleopatra in Act IV, sc. xiii. Her own death occurs in the next Act, after she has said half of line no. 315 "What should I stay—" in sc. ii.

Another most important point about the catastrophe of *AC* is the interpolation of the comic scene of the Clown. It is a long passage, extended over forty lines. The importance of this scene has at ready been pointed out, (*vide* Chap. 4, Act V, sc. ii, Chap IV and this Chap., certain Elizabethan features, *supra*). As has been observed already repeatedly, the death of Cleopatra is a glorious one and this has been differently interpreted by different critics. Some have considered it to be the most noble feature of the play and some to be a defect. Many critics consider the inclusion of a comic scene in the catastrophe with disapproval. But in this respect Bradley takes a positive view. According to him the introduction of this scene within the catastrophe is "the acme of audacity" but also that it is not incongruous with the mood of the play.

This is because Cleopatra knows and so do we, that Caesar will exhibit her and her children to the general public in his triumphal procession—a worse indignity than which can hardly be imagined. So she plans to triumph over him in death, and death in that case will be a glorious one—a victory over the victor. The audience does not yet know about the wonderful poetry that Shakespeare will give her after the exit of the Clown, but the mood is already heightened one:

> Show me, my women, like a queen, go fetch
> My best attires; I am again for Cydnus,
> To meet Mark Antony...
> ...Bring our crown and all.[30]

It is just at this moment that the old Clown comes. Bradley comments:

> The old countryman comes at a moment of tragic exaltation.... But the moment, though tragic, is emphatically one of exaltation. We have not been feeling horrified, nor are we feeling a dreadful suspense.[31]

The inclusion of the comic dialogue therefore is accepted with a calm mind and a smile by the audience and the reader. Indeed Una Ellis-Fermor expresses it most effectively when she says that this entire scene has:

> A solemn radiance that is wholly positive, the manifestation of that comprehension which, in its very nature, is beyond communication.... Beyond *AC* there is, it may be, no step further for tragedy to go.[32]

Among the several other features of the plot listed above, *Peripeteia* is definitely present in the case of both the hero and the heroine. Both are at the height of their glory in the beginning of the play and this state continues for quite some time. It is with his decision to fight at sea that his misfortunes begin (Act III, sc. vii). In the very next scene the disastrous defeat at Actium is reported by Enobarbus and Scarus. Six of the kings in his army and Canidius desert him.

Then his fortunes recover a little, if only for a short time. In Act IV, sc. vii in which he beats Agrippa's army and in sc. viii he is shown as elated with his triumph. Cleopatra greets him and he her:

Cleo.: Lord of lords!
O infinite virtue! com'st thou smiling from
The great word's snare uncaught?
Ant. : ...he hath fought today
As if a god, in hate of mankind, had
Destroy'd in such a shape.[33]

But this triumph is not an enduring one. In the next scene the unearthly music is heard which presages Hercules's leaving him. This makes one expect defeat in the next day's battle and that is what happens. Cleopatra, with her army, deserts him again and he is defeated and then she sends him the false message that she has committed suicide. His fortune is at its lowest ebb in this scene and he tries to kill himself:

...but I will be
A bridegroom in my death and run into't
As to a lover's bed.[34]

But, though he wounds himself mortally, he does not die here. Instead, when soon after this attempt he comes to know that Cleopatra is alive he has himself carried to her in her tower, and there, in the full glory of his tragic dignity, he meets his death. His dying speech shows him to be a victor:

Wherein I liv'd, the greatest prince o'the world,
The noblest; and now not basely die,
Not cowardly put off my helmet to
My countryman; a Roman by a Roman
Valiantly vanquish'd.[35]

Thus is *peripeteia* or the reversal of fortune completed. Aristotles definition of the ideal tragic plot is fully borne out: "a rather good man coming to a bad end."

The plot of *AC*, thus, shows the poet at a high point of his craft. Indeed, not only the plot, but the characters, style and all the other elements of drama show a very high degree of expertise in this play.

REFERENCES

1. Granville Barker, H., *op. cit.*, p. 86.
2. Butcher, S.H., *op. cit.*, pp. 27-29.

3. Hazlitt, in Brown, J.R., *op. cit.*, p. 33.
4. Granville-Barker, *op. cit.*, p. 93.
5. Bethell, S.L., *Shakespeare and the Popular Dramatic Tradition*, 1944, p. 116.
6. Dr. Johnson, *op. cit.*, p. 31.
7. Kronenberger, L., ed., *Alexander Pope: Selected Works*, New York, The Modern Library, 1951, pp. 353-54.
8. Act IV, sc. xii, ll. 44-47.
9. Butcher, S.H., *op. cit.*, pp. 95-97.
10. II : iii : 19-22.
11. II : iii : 25-28.
12. IV : iii : 16-17.
13. II : viii : 47-54.
14. V : ii : 271-75.
15. Bradley, A.C., *op. cit.*, p. 47.
16. Wain, *op. cit.*, p. 54.
17. Verity, A.W., Introduction to *Hamlet,* Cambridge, the University Press, Indian edn., 1989, pp. xx-xxi.
18. Bullough, G., p. 57.
19. *Ibid.*, pp. 302-03.
20. III : viii : 44-46.
21. Bullough, *op. cit.*, p. 298.
22. Bradley, *op. cit.*, p. 62.
23. Ellis-Fermor, U., *op. cit.*, p. 34.
24. I : ii : 136-38.
25. III : iii : 25-26.
26. Granville-Barker, *op. cit.*, pp. 95-96.
27. III : x : 51-66.
28. IV : x : 43-45.
29. Booth, Stephen, ed., *Shakespeare's Sonnets*, New Haven, Yale University Press, 1977, Son. no. 38.
30. V : III : 226-28.
31. Bradley, *op. cit.,* p. 334.
32. Ellis-Fermor, *op. cit.,* pp. 266-68.
33. IV : viii : 16-26.
34. IV : xiii : 99-101.
35. IV : xiii : 54-58.

9

Imagery in *AC*

Many stylistic devices are used by literary artists to give beauty to their work and make it all the more effective, and imagery is one of them. It is an important aspect of poetry, specially of drama, for the images a character uses reveal his personality, and carry out many other functions as well. Extensive as well as intensive studies of Shakespeare's imagery have been undertaken by many scholars, the foremost among them being Caroline Spurgeon and Wolfang Clemen. The development in his use of imagery, the function of his images, the relationship between the images and the characters using them, all these have been studied meticulously.

Images have been defined in many different ways by many different authors and critics. The one given by Henri Fluchère is particularly good.

> Imagery may shortly be defined as a concrete illustration drawn upon by the poet to clarify or embellish the object that he seeks to describe.[1]

Here the critic has mentioned only two functions—embellishment and clarifying. Shakespeare's images carry out many more, as for example anticipating future events, creating the atmosphere, expressing the mood of the character who is speaking and many others. His images are rarely just decorative, they are almost always functional.

It should always be kept in mind that often it is difficult, if not impossible, to distinguish between figures of speech, images and symbols. They often merge into each other. Usually an image is a figure of speech and sometimes it might reach the heights of a symbol. Fluchère does not neglect this trait:

> No strict rule allows us to say at what point we pass from the plane of pure rhetoric to the plane of pure psychology, and even the metaphysical plane in the use of imagery.[2]

Classification of images is not a simple task, for the same image can be considered under different categories. A sense image will also be a nature image or a domestic image or some other kind. This is a feature common to all images. Usually an image is first of all a sense image as everything is perceived through one sense or another, and then it belongs to some other kind according to the picture it gives, nature, etc.

Sense-images, thus, are the most important. There are five kinds of sense-images corresponding to our five senses. These are sight, hearing, smelling, tasting and touching. The corresponding senses are visual, auditory, olfactory, gustatory and tactile respectively. These will be mentioned now with reference to the text. Sense-images have a few features that are peculiar to them. The one and the same image may refer to different senses. Again, there is the technique known as synaesthesia in which an image that has special relevance for one sense is described in terms of another. Such special features are quite common in Shakespeare's poetry.

The images used in this play will now be taken up. As a detailed study is not possible, only a few obvious examples will be taken up to exemplify different kinds of images and the manner in which they have been used. First of all, to illustrate the use of sense-images, the famous description of Cleopatra by Enobarbus will be a very good starting-point. The entire picture of Cleopatra sitting in her barge, of course, is a visual image, but within this there are a host of other images. First of all there is the picture of the barge like a shining, floating throne:

> The barge she sat in, like a burnish'd throne,
> Burn'd on the water; the poop was beaten gold.[3]

This is, first of all, a visual image as the barge is presented as something to be seen. But in addition to this it is also an image of royalty ("throne") and a metal image as gold is mentioned. It is nautical image too, as a barge floating on the water is described. It goes on:

> Purple the sails and so perfumed, that
> The winds were love-sick with them.[4]

These one and a half lines have a host of images in them. The visual image is continued and added to because the colour of the sails is told to us. The nautical image too is continued, for sails are mentioned, and as they are "perfumed" the image develops olfactory features. Then, as sails are made of cloth or canvas one can say that it is a textile image too. In the next lines auditory image is added to these:

> The oars were silver
> Which to the tune of flutes kept stroke.[5]

So in these few lines (only five of them, so far) there are (a) visual, (b) auditory, (c) olfactory, (d) nautical, (e) textile, (f) metal images. Then, a few lines later we have:

> With diverse-colour'd fans, whose wind did seem
> To glow the delicate cheeks which they did cool.[6]

This, in addition to being a visual image is also a tactile one as it describes the effect of the wind touching her cheeks. Olfactory imagery is repeated a little later in another splendid image:

> From the barge
> A strange invisible perfume hits the sense.[7]

To make the passage even richer, classical or mythological images are also added to it:

> O'er-picturing that Venus which we see
> The fancy outwork nature; on each side her
> Stood pretty-dimpled boys like smiling cupids,
>
> ... ...
>
> Her gentlewomen, like the Nereides,
> So many mermaids, tended her i'the eyes.[8]

It would seem that the poet has covered all the senses save one, the sense of taste. But that is not the case. As the passage draws to a close, a very effective gustatory image crowns the entire description:

> Other women cloy
> The appetite they feed on, but she makes hungry
> Where most she satisfies.[9]

Thus in one passage (of course it is an extra rich one) he covers all the five senses repeatedly, then brings in nautical, metal, textile and classical images. But this is not all, for there is an extraordinary image which is very difficult to classify. He describes Antony sitting in the market-place and says that even the wind, if it were possible, would have gone to the bank of Cydnus to gaze at Cleopatra:

> Whistling to the air; which, but for vacancy,
> Had gone to gaze on Cleopatra too
> And made a gap in nature.[10]

This, as it refers to the air, will have to be called an element image. What is extraordinary about it is that it is a scientific image also, for it talks about the vacuum that would have been created if the air too had gone to see her.

All these images mentioned above come in one and the same passage, following quickly on the steps of each other. The passage, that is to say, is crowded with images. This kind of accumulation of images, which is a well-known feature of Shakespeare's poetry, gives it great complexity and richness.

These are all clear-cut and simple, obvious images. But Shakespeare's imagery is far more complex than this. There is, for example, what W. Clemen calls imagery-consciousness in which the image is implied, not explained:

> The image which is suggested is a further sign of the intensive penetration of the language by the "imagery-consciousness". The whole image is sunk beneath the surface, as it were, and has left behind it only one or two ideas concerned with it.[11]

There are a host of such implied images, evidence of the "imagery-consciousness" of Shakespeare's own consciousness. One such example is to be found in the very first speech itself:

> ...his captain's heart,
> Which in the scuffles of great fights hath burst

> The buckles on his breasts, reneges all temper,
> And is become the bellows and the fan
> To cool a gipsy's lust.[12]

Here the overall and dominant image is that of a bar of hot metal ("gipsy's lust") being cooled in the forge of a blacksmith ("bellow and the fan"). But this has not been clearly stated, it has to be inferred. Such hidden images are strewn all over the play. Clemen has said that in the mature plays of Shakespeare we often have to stop and ask "What image did Shakespeare here have in mind?" When such a question rises in the reader's mind it is evidence of the imagery consciousness of the poet's creative imagination.

Then there is the feature designated as "image-complex" by Caroline Spurgeon. This means the use of many images dealing with one implied idea which is not explained clearly. For example Shakespeare uses the image of gardening, but without talking directly about gardens uses just two or three related images. This shows a preference in his mind for:

> ...certain classes of things, certain qualities in things and certain aspects of life.[13]

Thus, gardening is one of the favourite topics in Shakespeare's imagery and there is one such in Enobarbus's prose speech when he hears of Fulvia's death:

> Your old smock brings forth a new petticoat; and indeed the tears live in an onion that should water this sorrow.[14]

Here there are only two words "bring forth" and "water" to make the image-complex of gardening clear to the reader. Sometimes such image-complexes are carried on for a few more lines, specially if the passage is in poetry.

When a certain image is repeated in many different way, throughout the book, it is called an "iterative" image. Such things have also been called "recurrent themes" and "recurrent motifs". Such phrases, respectively, refer to the theme and the style of a work. When it is used with reference to images it is called an "iterative image" and the term has been given by Caroline Spurgeon. There are many such creative images in the play under discussion and one of the most prevailing one is that of warfare. Images concerned with warfare, battles, etc. appear in the play from the very beginning and continue up till the end. Apart from images openly dealing with battles there are numerous oblique references to it:

(a) ...those his goodly eyes
That o'er the files and musters of the war
Have flowed like plated Mars.

(b) ....Sextus Pompeius
Hath given the dare to Caesar and commands
The empire of the sea.

(c) ....Upon your sword
Sit laughing victory! and smooth success
Be strew'd before your feet.

(d) ....But to confound such time
That drums him from his sport.

(e) And soberly did mount an arm-gaunt steed
Who neigh'd so high...[15]

These are only five oblique references to warfare only from the first Act. This will give the reader an idea of how many such images are there in the entire play. Besides these images oblique referring to warfare there are many clear-cut war images in the first Act alone. There are besides the war images, other iterative images in the play as well. One of them is image of the sea which are also present in the play from the beginning to the end, pervading the dialogue, as it were.

As far as the images prevailing in the play are concerned, both Caroline Spurgeon and W. Clemen have written in detail on them. As Clemen fully agrees with Spurgeon it will be advisable to look at his opinion since he not only agrees with her but adds to her opinion also. She, as well as he is of the opinion that there are certain images in *AC*.

> ...which strike the keynote of the play—the expanse of the world and the tremendous consciousness of power

> on the part of the characters—and which elevate the figures of these great rulers to the level of demi-gods.[16]

Then he proceeds to go through the play with these kinds of images in mind. He also points out that these images serve a double purpose: they give an impression of the characters' greatness and at the same time they create the atmosphere by giving the impression of a vast expanse of empire that includes oceans and seas, and not just land. To illustrate this point he takes one of the most magnificent images of the play, used by Antony to describe his might that has vanished now:

> I that with my sword
> Quarter'd the world, and O'er green Neptune's back
> With ships made cities.[17]

This is an image that adds to the status of Antony as a soldier, a man of physical valour ("I that with my sword") and also as a powerful ruler. "Quartering the world" gives an idea of the vastness of his empire and the mention of ships making cities proves his sovereignty over the seas. This image is taken from the scene a little before Antony tries to kill himself, but they occur in the beginning of the work too, when he is not recalling past grandeur but talking of the present. The word "world", as Caroline Spurgeon has noted, occurs 42 times in the play—a number which is double of that to be found in any other:

> The group of image in *AC* which, on analysis, immediately attract attention as peculiar to this play, consists of images of the world, the firmament, the ocean, and of vastness generally.[18]

The recurrent images of the heavenly bodies, like the sun and the moon and the stars also serve the same purpose. There are repeated descriptions of Antony relating him to the sun or to stars. In the very beginning of the play there is Philo's description of him has been quoted already. Then later Lepidus excuses his faults thus:

> His faults in him seem as the spots of heaven
> More fiery by night's blackness.[19]

Cleopatra's ecstatic description of him to Dolabella also relates him to stars:

> His face was as the heavens; and therein stuck
> A sun and moon which kept their course, and lighted
> The little O, the earth.[20]

All these images go to emphasize the grandeur of the character. Pointing this out, Clemen stresses the fact that such images are but symbolic representations of the characters they describe, they do not just create the atmosphere:

> (a) It is symbolically related to character, serves their self-interpretation and the expression of their feelings.
>
> (b) They reveal that Shakespeare viewed the lives of his great characters as being in harmony with the cosmic powers.[21]

In other words the images are not merely descriptive, they are functional as well. This is the case with the images in the mature plays. They have developed from the merely descriptive to dramatic or functional images as in *AC*.

Besides relating cosmic powers to human ones there is another very significant part played by imagery in *AC*—Anticipation of the future. Again and again, specially in this play, we come across images that are linked with destiny and give a foretaste of the future. This feature has been clearly pointed out by Clemen:

> The dramatic preparation of coming events in which images play a part is, in *AC*, pervaded by a strong sense of destiny.[22]

He calls them "imagery related to Fortune" and traces them from quite early in the play (Act I, sc. iii) with the words of the Soothsayer. Later when the same Soothsayer warns Antony in Rome it comes even more powerfully in evidence:

> If thou dost play with him at any game
> Thou art sure to lose...
> ...thy lustre thickens
> When he shines by.[23]

There are many images related to Fortune, specially in the second half of the play. In addition there is accumulation of images as there are no less than nine images in the five and half lines that have been quoted here.[24]

A later critic, M. Charney, has also studied the imagery of the play and has pointed out "three image themes". In other words, he has classified the images of the play into three divisions and is of the opinion that they recur in the play very much as themes do:

> ...tragic conflict between the values of Egypt and Rome and may be illustrated in three image themes: sword and armour, vertical dimension and dissolution.[25]

The images of sword and armour, as has already been pointed out in connection with "iterative imagery", is a predominant one in the play. It is the very first noticeable image that describes Antony. Philo describes him as "plated Mars" and two lines later speaks of his "captain's heart".

> Which in the scuffles of great fights hath burst
> The buckles on his breast.[26]

Charney points out that in a good part of the play Antony is in sword and armour and this helps the audience to visualize him as a mighty here:

> This is a presentation image of his role as a soldier and triumvir, his "royal occupation" (iv : iv : 17) and the verbal imagery helps to support this.[27]

In a way the use of sword and armour illustrates the tragic fall of Antony. This gains special attention in Act IV, sc. xii when he gets the false information of Cleopatra's death. Up till then, though in despair, he had been fully armed, in formal battle-dress. Now he starts to disarm:

> Unarm, Eros; the long day's task is done
> And we must sleep....
> .... Off, pluck off[28]

Though he had gained victory at first in the battle of three days, though he is such a renowned and valiant soldier, yet his own sword betrays him at the end, denying him the dignity of instant death. He fails to kill himself when he falls on his sword and has to die later not directly of a wound but through loss of blood.

The second image theme in the play is the "persistent imagery of vertical dimension". This is not difficult to understand as Antony and Cleopatra have been presented all along as being the highest in the world, and the rest of the world as being low:

> The basic pattern here is the contrast in vertical dimension between the high and the low, up and down.[29]

This critic however, lays more stress on physical height and lowness than on imagery. For example he points out that when defeated at Actium Antony sits down and stands up only after being repeatedly asked by Eros. There are many other references to the height and lowness of characters and their station in life with reference to Antony and Cleopatra. At the end of his career he has fallen very low indeed, in comparison with Caesar. Yet paradoxically it is this fall that gives him a different kind of height—a height to which Caesar never attains. It is the height of tragic dignity and Charney points out that in the play this is made clear in a physical sense as well for he is lifted up to the monument in the death-scene:

> The action "They heave Antony aloft to Cleopatra" (IV: xv : 37) presents a literal image of height in the use of the upper stage.... The theatre thus provides us with a metaphor of elevation for his death.[30]

This is the ultimate height to which Antony attains, a height that can be reached, paradoxically only by those who have, in a wordly sense, fallen down. Tragic dignity is not easy to attain.

The third image theme is the theme of dissolution. The most effective example that this critic gives is that of the supernatural music the soldiers hear in Act IV, sc. iii. What happens in this scene is this: there are three soldiers on duty on the eve of the second day's battle and they suddenly hear an unearthy music. The stage direction says that it comes from "under the stage" and the soldiers also say it is coming from "under the earth":

> *1st sol.* : What should this mean?
>
> *2nd sol.*: 'Tis the god Hercules, whom Antony lov'd
> Now leaves him.[31]

No one contradicts him, so it can be taken that this is what Shakespeare means it to represent. This is the herald of the defeat that is in store for Antony. This critic gives a very suggestive interpretation of this phenomenon:

> This scene is in the symbolic tradition of the mediaeval pageant wagon, when the stage itself represented the world, with heaven above and hell below.[32]

The theme of dissolution had been present before this also, and will be present after this too, but Charney finds this instance to be the best illustration of it.

It can be clearly seen that Shakespeare's imagery is of a very complex and rich variety, yielding new treasures of significance the more it studied and analysed. Like all his other arts, that is, characterization, versification, etc. this aspect of his drama also developed more and more as he himself matured, so that there is significant difference between the way imagery has been used in *A Midsummer Night's Dream* and the way it has been used in *AC*. As W. Clemen says:

> The imagery eventually become the favourite mode of expression of the later Shakespeare.[33]

REFERENCES

1. Fluchère, H, *op. cit.*, p. 167.
2. *Ibid.*
3. Act II: sc. ii : ll. 199-200.
4. II : ii : 201-02.
5. II : ii : 202-03.
6. II : ii : 211-12.
7. II : ii : 220-21.
8. II : ii : 208-15.
9. II : ii : 244-46.
10. II : ii : 224-26.
11. Clemen, W., *The Development of Shakespeare's Imagery*, Lond, Methuen and Co., 1977, p. 77.
12. I : i : 6-10.
13. Spurgeon, E., *Shakespeare's Imagery and What it tells Us,* Combr. Univ. Press, 1935, p. 44.

14. I : ii : 80-82.
15. (a) I : i : 2-4, (b) I : ii : 196-98, (c) I : iii : 99-101, (d) I : iv : 28-29, (e) I : v : 48-49.
16. Spurgeon, E., *op. cit.*, p. 350.
17. IV : xii : 57-59.
18. Spurgeon, E., *op. cit.* p. 350.
19. I : iv : 12-13
20. V : ii : 79-81.
21. Clemen W., *op. cit.*, (a) p. 162, (b), p. 165.
22. *Ibid.*, p. 165.
23. II : iii : 25-28.
24. IV : xiii : 2-8.
25. Charney, M., *The Imagery of Antony and Cleopatra* in Brown, J.R. *op. cit.*, p. 140.
26. I : i : 7-8.
27. Charney, op. cit., p. 141.
28. IV : xii : 35-37.
29. *Op. cit.*, p. 146.
30. *Ibid.*, p. 147.
31. IV : iii : 15-17.
32. *Op. cit.*, p. 149.
33. *Op. cit.*, p. 5.

10

Poetic Style: Diction and Versification

There are two aspects to which attention has to be paid while reading poetry: the thoughts and the emotions expressed, and the style. It is but to be expected that the poetic style of our poet should be studied in great detail. Not only does his style reflect his age, it being an Elizabethan-Jacobean style, but it reflects his own individual approach as well. Yet the style is suited to each of the characters. Such an achievement, though difficult, is not impossible, as can be seen in our poet.

Elizabethan plays were written in a mixture of prose and poetry. The noble character, who usually featured in the main plot, spoke in verse and the humble ones in prose. This was not an inflexible rule for there were many exceptions to it. Poetic style, moreover, is a phrase covering both the language and the versification of a play. Both of these will now be studied.

(A) POETIC DICTION

Diction is an aspect of poetry that has been studied in detail from classical times onwards. The Elizabethans were familiar with these theories, specially those of the Roman theorists. Horace in his *Ars Poetica* had put down clear-cut rules about poetic diction. The diction of different kinds of poetry should be different and so should that of dramatic characters in a play. In drama the characters should speak in conformity with their (a) age, (b) sex, and (c) their position in life:

> It will make a great difference whether a god or a hero is speaking, a man of ripe years or a hot-headed

> youngster in the pride of youth, a woman of standing or an officious nurse, a roaming merchant or a prosperous farmer.[1]

This long and famous sentence provides for all possibilities, from superhuman characters to humble pedlars. A god or a hero must not speak like ordinary characters. Among ordinary human beings, again, there are many varieties and each on should be given the language most suited to him. Age, sex and social status, all have been considered by Horace in the examples he gives within these basic categories. Again, there are many other differences, particularly so far as social position is concerned. These categories can be added to *ad infinitum*, and each individual has to speak the language that is the most natural to him. These differences were scrupulously observed in later Elizabethan drama. M.C. Bradbrook commenting upon the intricacies of style in the drama of this period observes:

> The specific style for princes, for lovers, for clowns, was fixed.[2]

But whatever variety of style the poet is using, he should keep certain general rules in mind—The diction, first of all, must be in keeping with the speaker's personality. It must also be able to move the reader or the audience emotionally:

> The Elizabethan dramatist's style is one of impassioned poetic rhetoric, the two commonest functions of which are to persuade and to touch the emotions.[3]

In addition to these requirements there is another basic one pointed out by classical theorists: a poet should make use of rhetorical devices. Aristotle, as may be seen in the definition already given (*vide* Chap. 8, *supra*) has specifically mentioned that the language of tragedy should be properly embellished according to the situation. Whether the style is of the grand, or the middle, or the low variety, figures of speech should be there. Ben Jonson's *The Alchemist* has an aristocrat in Sir Epicure Mammon who speaks in the grand manner, and it has got a servant in Face and a prostitute in Dol Common who speak the low style. All however, use figures of speech. Jonson is very particular about this.

In addition to classical theorists, there were English ones as well. They, followed the classical theories. George Puttenham is the best-known. He is emphatically in favour of an ornamental diction:

> There is nothing so fitte for the poem as to be furnished with el the figures that be Rhetoricall and such as do most beautifie the language with eloquence.[4]

The classical and the Renaissance scholars have expounded many theories of diction. Among the classical theorists Horace has been the most influential. In his famous theory of poetic diction he has given many important rules, some of which have been mentioned above. He, moreover, advocates the use of newly-coined words as well as out-of-mode ones. Shakespeare was fully familiar with classical as well as contemporary rules and conventions and used them, or not, according to his own convenience. The style of *AC* is a very mature one:

(i) Diction in AC

The two decades that contain the best of our poet's work show continuous development of all the elements of drama. Style, imagery, dramatic strategy, stage-craft, all went on developing from one play to the next, right till the very end. *AC* is a work of his mature artistry and in it he has used the kind of diction that is eminently suited to the kind of play it is—a historical tragedy. Derek Traversi comments thus on the style of these plays:

> The style of these plays, far from reflecting a pedestrian process of versification, shows a unique combination of narrative lucidity, achieved through the easy, almost conversational use of speech rhythms and vernacular phrases, to poetic intensities that flow effortlessly from this foundation whenever the state of action so allows.[5]

Shakespeare uses conversational rhythms and phrases and elevates them to "poetic intensities" not just in this play but in others also. In addition he uses all the contemporary conventions as well.

Like all the other dramatists of his time he too has made use of both prose and verse. He uses them not merely to indicate the social position of the speakers but also to heighten or lower the pitch of the dialogue. Even his noble characters use prose from time to time, but turn to poetry when a loftier or serious tone is needed. This device can be applied not just to the use of prose and verse but to all kinds of style for the diction, as Aristotle has pointed out, must suit not just the character but the situation as well:

> ....Language enriched in a variety of ways and artistic devices appropriate to several parts of the play.[6]

This actually means that even the same character must not speak in the same manner in all the different situations in the play. Yet, whoever it is who speaks and in whatever situation, the style, besides suiting the character and the occasion, always gives forth a sense of power. Coleridge, with the great insight of a great critic, had pointed it out first:

> *Feliciter audax* is the motto for its style comparatively with his other works.... Be it remembered too that this happy valiancy of style is but the representative and result of all the material excellencies so exprest.[7]

(ii) Stylistic Devices

There are many stylistic devices to heighten the efficacy of poetic diction. Imagery, symbolism and figures of speech are the most important of these. Imagery has already been discussed in the preceding chapter and some of the most obvious figures of speech used in *AC* will be taken up now.

Simile, metaphor, alliteration and pun are the most obvious figures of speech that strike the reader first and all of them are to be found in abundance in this play. There is a remarkable simile in the very first speech of the play:

> That o'er the files and musters of the war.
> Have glow'd like plated Mars.[8]

Philo is here comparing Antony with Mars the god of war in full armour ("plated"). The simile not only adds majesty to Antony but makes his prowess as warrior clear.

Homeric similes are those that are continued for a few lines and there is one in Enobarbus's prose speech when he receives the news that Antony is going to go to Rome:

> We cannot call her words and waters sighs and tears; they are greater storms and tempests than almanacs can report: this cannot be cunning in her; if it be, she makes a show of rain as well as Jove.[9]

Homeric similes are not very common even in poetry, and here is one in prose. Then again such figures of speech occur usually in serious poetry, and here it is found in humorous, if not scornful, prose. Both of these features are unusual.

Metaphors are of many kinds and they are strewn generously all along the play. One occurs in the very beginning of the play in Philo's scornful description of Antony:

> You shall see in him
> The triple pillar of the world transform'd
> Into a strumpet's fool.[10]

As a metaphor this is a simple one, but this is not the case always. Very often the metaphor is an implied one, a hidden or frozen metaphor where the reader has to stop and think:

> The present pleasure,
> By revolution lowering, does become
> The opposite of itself.[11]

Here we have the hidden or frozen metaphor of a wheel turning so that the point which is uppermost easily becomes the lowermost one. Such metaphors, as is quite apparent, can also be taken as examples of "imagery consciousness" as given by Caroline Spurgeon and W. Clemen (*vide* Chap. 9 *supra*).

Mixed metaphors are usually employed to produce comic effects. They are rarely used in serious poetry. But there is an example of a mixed metaphor being used by Antony in a serious mood:

> O! then we bring forth weeds
> When our quick winds lie still.[12]

Here in the first line the metaphor used is one of gardening and in the second of sailing. Both describe the same thing: a man's reaction to bad news. This is an uncommon example of a mixed metaphor used in serious poetry.

Figures of speech that might not be so obvious are apparent everywhere. A good example of synecdoche is to be found in the scene in which Antony, before starting for Rome bids farewell to Cleopatra. She, as she bids him farewell, wishes him success:

> Upon your sword
> Sit laurel victory! and smooth success
> Be strew'd before your feet![13]

Here at first a sword, i.e. a concrete object, is substituted for Antony's valour, which is an abstract thing and then success is compared with flowers strewn before his feet, i.e. success, an abstract thing, is substituted for the concrete object flower. Then again, repeatedly in the play Cleopatra is addressed as and referred to as Egypt and this is a case of metonymy, for an entire country is substituted for one of its products, an individual.

Tautology is included within the group of figures of sound and there is a very fine instance of one to be found in the farewell scene referred to above. It is used by Cleopatra:

> Sir, you and I must part, but that's not it:
> Sir, you and I have lov'd, but that's not it:[14]

This figure of speech is often used for emphasis and that is how it has been used in this speech.

But picking up instances of different kinds of rhetorical devices cannot give any impression of the grandeur of poetry in the play. It is like making the same mistake for which Dr. Johnson had criticised the metaphysical poets. Speaking of the analytical method of these poets he says that they cannot give an overall picture of anything, any more than a person:

> ...who dissects a sunbeam with a prism can exhibit the wide effulgence of a summer noon.[15]

This is the reason why the analysis of at least one passage from the point of view of rhetoric is necessary. This analysis will present only one aspect and not the overall poetic effect of the entire passage. It is one of the passages in which Cleopatra is lamenting the death of Antony. There are several such passages and this is the first of them. It begins just before Antony's death and continuous after it, for during this speech Antony dies, and Cleopatra, half-demented with grief, continues:

> Noblest of men, woo't die?
> Hast thou no care of me? Shall I abide
> In this dull world, which in thy absence is
> No better than a sty? O! see my women,
> (Antony *dies*)
> The crown o' the earth doth melt. My lord!
> O! wither'd is the garland of the war,
> The soldier's pole is fall'n; young boys and girls
> Are level now with men; the odds is gone,
> And there is nothing left remarkable
> Beneath the visiting moon. (Swoons)[16]

First of all, the entire passage is an apostrophe, for it is addressed to Antony. Some might say it is an invocation, but in an invocation the person or the entity addressed is requested to do something, which is not the case here. Then right in the beginning of it there are three rhetorical questions, coming one upon the other. Then Cleopatra addresses her women "O! see my women." This is an exclamation. Deep grief is expressed through this exclamation. Then, since Cleopatra is asking her women to see something that is not present there to be perceived by the physical sense of sight, she is presenting a picture to be seen with the eye of imagination: "The crown o' the earth doth melt". This, therefore, is the figure of speech known as vision, not a very well-known figure. Both "the crown o' the earth" and "the garland of the war" are metaphors, emphasizing the beauty and the valour of Antony. "The soldier's pole is fall'n", in addition to being a metaphor is also a synecdoche because in it the part (the pole) represents the whole (the flag carried by a soldier). One can also call it a metonymy, for here the symbol (the flag) is used for the thing symbolized (valour in war). In the phrase "the odds is gone" we have metonymy again, for "odds" stands for the wager. Finally in "the visiting moon" there is personification of the moon. Thus in a passage of ten lines there are as many figures of speech.

This kind of analysis, however, does not tell us anything about the poetic value of the passage. Moreover, even if one does not know or care about the figures of speech, sublime poetry can still be enjoyed. The student should not allow himself to attach undue importance to this kind of analysis, though it is necessary for scholarly purposes. An analysis of this kind also helps one to realize the complexity of Shakespeare's style, for it looks only at one aspect—the rhetorical one, and at nothing else. If the imagery, etc. are analysed, new beauties will be seen.

(B) VERSIFICATION

As has been pointed out above, poetic style has two aspects to it: the diction and the versification. A discussion of style should pay attention to both in order to be complete. The technique of versification should be studied. This aspect of poetry is usually considered to be highly technical but it is not a purely technical matter, for it affects the emotional response of the reader and the audience. Henri Fluchère has pointed out:

> It is by its rhythm as much as by its image that a verse is expressive. The rhythmical succession has an emotional pattern, shows a purpose imposing a mood or defining a thought.[17]

The customary poetic form of late Elizabethan drama was blank verse, with couplets in frequent use Blank verse is a passage of unrhymed iambic pentametre lines. Lambic is a disyllabic metre, in which the first syllable is weak (or unstressed, or short) and the second is strong (or stressed or long), as for example:

> Ŏ wí/ thĕr'd íś/the gár/ lañd óf/ the wár,
> The sól/ dieř's pole/iš fall'n/; yoŭng bóys/ añd girls
> Aře lé/vĕl nów/ with/ mén/; thĕ odds /iš góne
> Añd thére/ iš nó/ thing left/remár/ kăble[18]

There are four lines here, not rhyming in any way. All the feet are iambics, for each line has exactly ten syllables, i.e. five feet. That is to say, this is a passage of entirely regular blank verse. Such absolutely regular passages of blank verse are quite rare, for usually there are many, many kinds of variations and irregularities used by the poet in order to avoid monotony as well as to give the actor more liberty in declaiming the passages.

Such irregularities are of many kinds, a few of which may be mentioned here. One of them is the use of end-stopped and run-on lines. In the passage given above, for example, there is a comma at the end of the first line, so that the actor will have to pause there for a little time. Such lines are end stopped lines. On the other hand, the lines run on to the next in the passage given below:

> The miserable change now at my end
> Lament nor sorrow at; but please your thoughts
> In feeding them with those my former fortunes
> Wherein I liv'd, the greatest prince o' the world.[19]

Here the actor will not stop at the end of the line, but will go on delivering the next without any break, making an emphatic pause at the comma in the fourth line. These are run-on lines. They usually make for a smooth flow whereas end-stopped lines give a jerky movement. But a poet, can use stopped lines in order to enhance the naturalness and the beauty of his verse. There is an entire passage spoken by Octavia:

> O my good Lord!
> Believe not all; or, if you must believe,
> stomach not all. A more unhappy lady,
> If this division chance, ne'er stood between,
> Praying for both parts,[20]

Here, because of the pause at the end, every line gets emphasis. Octavia is very agitated and speaks most emphatically, stressing each line. The passage is effective because each line is an end-stopped one.

Blank verse lines usually have a brief pause in them known as the caesura or the medial pause. The placing of the pause within the line is an important factor in versification for the flexibility of the passage will depend, to a large extent, on this factor. In medieval verse the caesura used to be placed in the middle of the line which used to give the entire poem an artificial rhythm. This should be avoided in drama at all costs, unless of course, the writer wants to produce some special effects. The Elizabethan dramatist would consider the actor's convenience and place the caesura accordingly:

> The crown o' the earth doth melt. // My lord!
> O! // wither'd is the garland of the war,
> The soldier's pole is fall'n; // Young boys and girls
> Are level now with men; // the odds is gone.[21]

As should be quite clear, the poet has himself indicated the pause in the line by giving punctuation marks. The double vertical lines indicate the caesura. If the syllables are counted, the caesura is seen to fall thus:

> 1st line–after the seventh syllable.
>
> 2nd line–after the first syllable.
>
> 3rd line–after the sixth syllable.
>
> 4th line–after the sixth syllable.

This positional change of the caesura has given a very great flexibility to the rhythm, bringing it near to the rhythm of speech. At times, in order to produce special effects, there may be more than one caesura in a line. Thus when the dying Antony is brought to Cleopatra she asks those around her to pull him up to her room in the monument:

> Antony//Antony!//Help,//Charmian,//help,//Iras,//help.[22]

This is an extreme case where there is a pause after every word. Cleopatra is panting and stopping after each word for she is hauling Antony up.

Blank verse, by definition, means that there should be ten syllables to a line. This rule, however, is not an inflexible one. A line may often have more than ten syllables in it. The line below, for example, has eleven:

> Ŏf lífe /ăt ónce/ŭntíe; /poŏr vé/nŏmóus/ foŏl[23]

Sometimes there are even longer ones, containing twelve syllables, which makes it an Alexandrine:

> Whĭch ís / my̆ héa /vén tŏ / háve.
> Cóme/thŏu mór/tăl wórm[24]

Just as these two lines are a bit longer than a pentametre so there might be shorter ones too. Short lines can be used most effectively:

Mec. Now Antony must leave her utterly.

Enobar. Never; he will not:

Age cannot wither her nor custom stale.[25]

Here Enobarbus's first line has only five syllables—it is half the length of a normal blank verse line. This is what has made the line so very effective.

This brief discussion has perhaps made it clear that good dramatic blank verse can never be absolutely regular iambic pentametre. There are many other metrical devices that lend the flexibility of speech rhythm to dramatic blank verse. One of them is stichomythia which will now be explained.

Without dialogues a play cannot be a play and often enough a line is broken up between two or more speakers to avoid monotony. It is used very often:

Ant: The queen shall then have courtesy, so she will yield us up?

Euph.: He says so.

Ant.: Let her know't.[26]

Here one pentametre line is broken into three parts by two speakers speaking, in all, three time. But the line is to be counted as one, a pentametre. Sometimes a line is broken into four parts by putting three breaks:

Cleo. : Octavia?

Mess. : Ay, Dread queen.

CL.: Where?

Mess.: Madam, in Rome.[27]

Sometimes two or more speakers speak quickly after each other, capping up each other's lines, rather like cross-talk. This device is usually to be found in comedies. But it can be found in more serious contexts than comic ones. Antony's admirers speak about him:

Eno.: A very fine one. O! how he loves Caesar.
Agr.: Nay, but how dearly he adores Mark Antony!
Eno.: Caesar! Why, he's the Jupiter of men.
Agr.: What is Antony? The god of Jupiter.
Eno.: Spake you of Caesar? How! the nonpareil!
Agr.: O, Antony! O thou Arabian bird![28]

Even though the staple metre of a play is blank verse, couplets too are used by the dramatists. It is used most often at the end of scenes or Acts. Usually such couplets sum up the theme of the scene and often give the emotional attitude of the character who is speaking it. Such couplets, coming at the ends of long passages or scenes or Acts often point out a moral such couplets are known as Senecan "sentences" because Seneca used them to point out moral lessons. The one given below, however, is not a Senecan couplet:

That thou residing here, go'st yet with me,
And I hence fleeting, hence remain with thee.[29]

This couplet does not point out a moral. Instead it sums up the conclusion reached by Antony after he has bidden farewell to Cleopatra. There is a rather odd couplet a bit earlier in this scene which is also a case of tautology [*vide* section (i) above]. The lines are rhyming ones, and more or less the same words have been used. It is Cleopatra who says it, bidding farewell to Antony:

Sir, you and I must part, but that's not it:
Sir, you and I have lov'd, but there's not it:[30]

A word should here be said about the songs in the plays. So far as this feature goes, *AC* is but a poor play, for there is just one song in it. Since there are so many love-scenes in it and the protagonists are archetypal lovers more songs could have been expected, especially in the first half of the play. But the play does not fulfil these expectations, for there is just one song in it and that is not a love song. It is a drinking song and occurs in the feast scene (Act II, sc. iii) and as such, is a ritual song. There are not many songs like this in his plays.

It used to be the Roman custom to pay homage to the god Bacchus, who is the god of wine, towards the end of a feast.

The man who was the most drunk used to be solemnly adorned with a wreath and greeted as Bacchus. A song and dance often used to accompany this ritual. Here also Enobarbus makes the guests join hands and dance in a ring while this song is sung, though no one is crowned as Bacchus. It is a very simple drinking song in trochaic tetrametre couplets. The peculiarity lies in the fact that every line is catalectic, i.e., short of one weak syllable at the end:

> Cóme/thŏu mónarĭch /óf the/vine
> Plúmpў/Bacchŭs / wíth piňk /éyne[31]

This device is often used in short songs of this type. There are quite a few drinking songs in Shakespeare, but none like thus, addressed directly to the god of wine and accompanied by a dance.

Poetic style, in its many different aspects, is but one of the facets of a play, albeit a very important one. From the very few examples given here the earnest reader will easily guess at the enormous variety of imagery and rhetorical figures that are scattered throughout the play. As for versification, A.C. Bradley is of the opinion that in *AC* it has reached a new peak:

> The versification, by the time we reach *AC,* has assumed a new type...it is always full of life and movement, and in great passages produces sudden, strange, electrifying effects which are rarely found in earlier plays...*AC,* in which Shakespeare's final style first shows itself practically complete.[32]

REFERENCES

1. Dorsch, T.S., ed. and transl., *Classical Literary Criticism,* Penguin Books, 1975, p. 83.
2. Brabbrook, M.C., *op. cit.*, p. 45.
3. Fluchère, H., *op. cit.*, p. 152.
4. Quoted in *ibid.*, p. 159.
5. Traversi, D., *op. cit.*, p. 10.
6. Dorsch, T.S., *op. cit.*, p. 39.
7. Coleridge, in Brown, J.R., *op. cit.*, p. 29.

8. Act I : sc. i : ll. 3-4.
9. I : ii : 157-62.
10. I : ii : 11-63.
11. I : ii : 133-35.
12. I : ii : 118-19.
13. I : iii : 99-101.
14. I : iii : 87-88.
15. Brady, F. and Wimsatt, W.K. ed., *Samuel Johnson: Selected Poetry and Prose*, N.Y. and New Haven, Univ. of California, 1975, p. 349.
16. IV : xiii : 59-68.
17. Fluchère, *op. cit.*, p. 181.
18. IV : xiii : 64-69.
19. IV : xiii : 51-54.
20. IV : xiii : 64-69.
21. IV : xiii : 63-66.
22. IV : xiii : 12.
23. V : ii : 306.
24. V : ii : 305.
25. II : ii : 241-43.
26. III : xi : 16.
27. III : iii : 8.
28. III : ii : 7-12.
29. I : iii : 103-04.
30. I : iii : 87-88.
31. II : vii : 120-21.
32. Bradey, A.C., *op. cit.*, pp. 68-69.

11

Critical Reception: A Brief History

AC, though written at the height of Shakespeare's mature art, has never been as popular as for example, *Julius Caesar*. It was written late in 1606 or quite early in 1607. The same year Samuel Daniel wrote a new edition of his own tragedy *Cleopatra* which shows influences of Shakespeare's play. Dryden's *All for Love* revived interest in the play as he openly acknowledged his debt to Shakespeare, specially in the style:

> In my style I have professed to imitate the divine Shakespeare.... I may offer and without vanity, that by imitating him, I have excelled myself.[1]

Garrick had revived a modified version in 1759, and shortly after this Dr. Johnson published his edition of the play with a brief note. This was the very first serious literary criticism. He praised the quick action in the play, though he noted a deficiency in character delineation:

> The continuous hurry of the action, the quick succession of one personage to another, call the mind forward without intermission from the first Act to the last.[2]

Serious literary criticism can be said to have begun from the nineteenth century, with A.W. Schlegel and Hazlitt. Both have been quoted repeatedly in the foregoing pages. They consider the play as a historical tragedy as indeed the later Danish critic Georg Brandes was also to do. Both Schlegel and Brandes point out the difficulties and excellence of the play as a historical tragedy (*vide* Chap. 3, *supra)*. Hazlitt's study of the play consider it from many different angles like the genre, character drawing, plot, style, etc. Coleridge's comments on the play are available in the form of short notes and he laid stress upon the style:

> ...in all exhibitions of a giant power in its strength and vigour of maturity.... *Feliciter audax* is the motto for its style...this happy valiancy of style is but the representation and result of all the material excellence so exprest.[3]

Dowden's study of the play, like Hazlitt's, considers all the different features of the play: the character, the theme, the plot, etc. He compares the portrait, of Cleopatra with that of Delilah in Milton's *Samson Agonistes*. Swinburne's study of the play is remarkable chiefly for its ecstatic praise of Cleopatra whom he finds incomparable:

> From her first imperial dawn on the stage of Shakespeare to the setting of that eastern star behind a pall of undissolved cloud we feel the charm and the terror and the mystery of her absolute and royal soul.[4]

Both in stage performance as in literary criticism the twentieth century saw great enthusiam in every field. Stage performance was encouraged because of its very nature—it being a costume play of great spectacles and great charm. Serious literary criticism in the last century can be said to have begun with A.C. Bradley who, though he omitted it from his *Shakespearean Tragedy*, wrote a comprehensive chapter on it in his *Oxford Lectures on Poetry* (1909). His opinions have been repeatedly quoted and discussed and explained in the earlier chapters of this book in different contexts.

After this Shakespearean criticism itself proliferated to a very great extent. It branched out in several directions. Twentieth-century Shakespearean criticism is roughly divisible into three categories: (a) interest in contemporary thought and life, (b) interest in diction and imagery, (c) interest in theatrical technique. The first of these include a study of the sources of Shakespeare's play, best exemplified by G. Bullough's monumental work *Narrative and Dramatic Sources of Shakespeare,* and works by Theodore Spencer, Lily B. Compbell,

Willard Farnham and many others. Bullough's work has been repeatedly referred to, but he concentrates more on the plot and characters than on the philosophical aspects of the play. Theodore Spencer, on the other hand, places Shakespeare's play against the perspective of traditional theories of man and his place in the universe and judges them from that point of view. The following sentence will make it clear

> By a fresh use of the three inter-related hierarchies of Nature, the world and the state, Shakespeare gave to this play the breadth and size which his vision of the subject demanded, and which was so much richer than anything he found in Plutarch.[5]

This branch of criticism has continued well into the later decades of the century, as for example in Leonard Tennenhouse's study of the political attitude in the play: *Power on Display* (1986).

The inquiries into the language and imagery of the play have given rise to a very prolific branch of criticism for critics have not only studied the style and the imagery, but have interpreted the play in their light. Caroline Spurgeon's *Shakespeare's Imagery* (1936) and W.H. Clemen's *The Development of Shakespeare's Imagery* (1951) study the imagery in detail but they do not base the interpretation of the play's different elements on this to the extent that G. Wilson Knight and J. Middleton Murry do. Wilson Knight in his *The Imperial Theme* (1931) collects significant words in the play and proceeds to give a philosophical interpretation of it in the light of these words. Murry also lays great emphasis on the poetry and studies certain significant words like "royalty", "loyalty" and some others and comes to the conclusion:

> We cannot just judge a play such as this as a record of action merely; if we do, its essence escapes our judgement.[6]

Apart from these there have been many others following the different schools of literary criticism as they sprang up during the twentieth century. Thus there have been psychological criticism e.g. Kay Stockholder's interpretation of Cleopatra as a mother figure and Antony's "Oedipal crime".

Marxism, Freudianism and Feminism came into vogue during the first part of the last century. Criticism following these theories have continued well into the present century but in addition, specially after the second world war other schools of literary criticism came into existence, e.g. structuralism and post-structuralism, colonialism and postcolonialism, modernism and post-modernism, etc. They have all tried their hands at Shakespearean criticism, but whether they have tackled this play in particular has not been possible to ascertain.

In India there has been a new development in the study of Shakespeare in the light of Sanskrit aesthetics. There are many ancient Sanskrit critical theories: Dhvani, Alaṅkāra, Rasa and others. Of late a study of Shakespeares's comedies in the light of Rasavāda has been published. Tragedies have also been studied in the same manner, like *Romeo and Juliet*, *Othello*, etc. A few years ago a study of *AC* in the light of Rasavāda had been published. This will be given in brief now, detailed study is not possible here.

Indian Interpretation

In his authoritative book on drama *Daśa-rūpa ka Ācārya* Dhananjaya classifies plays or *rūpakas* into ten kinds. This division has been done in accordance with the different kinds of story—continuity, characters and the *aṅgī rasa* in mind:

> *Vastu, netā, rasāṣṭenaṅ bhedako vastu ca dvidhā*[7].—
> That is to say, plays differ in three things—the subject-matter, the hero and the rasa (unless otherwise indicated, the translations are by the present writer).

This play can be called a *nāṭaka* as the story as well as the characters are taken from history (*prakhyāta*). Nearly all the characteristics of a *nātaka* as given by Dhananjaya can be found in it. In addition to the fact that both the theme and the characters are *prakhyāta* or well-known, so far as the structure goes it is as if Shakespeare had consciously followed Dhananjaya's dictum:

> *Ādyantamevam niścitya pañcadhā tadvibhājya ca*[8]
>
> —The entire play should be decidedly divided into five parts from the beginning till the end.

As far as the question of *rasa* goes Dhananjaya has clearly ruled:

> Eko rasoangīkartavyo vīrah śṛṅgāra eva vā[9]
>
> Only one *rasa* should predominate, whether it be *vīra* or *śṛṅgāra*.

In this play *śṛṅgāra* is the main or the *aṅgī* rasa, with *vīra* as the most important of the supporting rasas. The main theme is love, so *śṛṅgāra* or the Erotic is the *angī* here. It fulfills the three requirements of the *angī*: *Vahuvyapti* (greatness of range), *Pātrodyama* (impelling the protagonist) and *phālagama* (the end result). It is present from the beginning to the very end of the play, so the condition of *Vahuvyāpti* is fulfilled and a more detailed study will show that the actions of the hero and the heroine are motivated by love, Antony's following the fleeing Cleopatra at Actium being the most obvious example. Thus the second requirement has also been met. As far as *phalāgama* is concerned it might be objected that the proper end in a play with love as the theme should be the union of the lovers, but here it is the opposite—they are united in the beginning of the play and separated for ever at the end. But though the play ends with death there can be no doubt that they are united in their death and there is a mood of exaltation as has already been pointed out (*vide* Chaps. 3 and 5, *supra*). Indeed Caesar stresses this union.

> She shall be buried by her Antony:
> No grave upon the earth shall clip in it
> A pair so famous.[10]

The ending of this play, more than that of any other, illustrates the fact that *Karuṇa rasa* can produce a deep joy. *Ācārya* Abhinavagupta says:

> Asmanmate samavedanāmeva ananda-ghanam-āsvādyate. Tatra kā duhkhāśaṅka?[11]
>
> —According to me the experience through sympathy is full of bliss. Where is the fear of sorrow in such an experience?

The influence of love is so strong that when, Dryden dramatized the same story he called it *All for Love.*

Looking at the characters, Antony approaches the *dhīra-lalita* hero the nearest. It might be objected that the Antony of *Julius Caesar* appears as a warrior, how then can he be *dhīra-lalita* here? This is because in this play he appears mainly as a lover. He neglects his duties and is utterly infatuated. Even his own followers admit the fact. So, indeed, does he. Again and again he says that he must break the bonds of love. It is true that he reveals himself as a warrior in the second half of the play. But this does not prevent him from excelling as a *dhīra-lalita* hero. As Dhananjaya says that all heroes in general, should be *śūro dṛdhaśca tejaśvī* (heroic, determined and forceful). In addition the *dhiralalita* is, Dhananjaya tells us:

Niścinto dhīra-lalitah kalāsakta sukhī mṛdu.[12]

Such a hero is also eloquent and humorous. There is at least one scene in which the witty aspect of Antony is seen. In Act II, sc. vii he becomes witty at the expense of Lepidus's drunkenness. The relevant lines have been quoted already. The humour evinced in the dialogue might be considered to be cheap and also unworthy of Shakespeare as well as of Antony. But it must be remembered that it is not meant to provoke pure laughter. It is satirical, for it shows Antony's contempt for, and lack of respect for Lepidus.

Cleopatra is a *pragārha-yauvana, pragalbhā* and *adhīrā* heroine—mature, forthcoming and impatient. Different scenes present different facets of her nature. If we think of the eight *nāyika* classification it becomes clear at once that she is a *svādhīna-bhaṛtrkā* heroine, in the scenes where she is with Antony. In the scenes of separation she is a *Proṣita-bhartṛkā.* The best aspects of her character are revealed in the death-scene where, like an *abhisārikā* she dresses herself for her last tryst with Antony.

Not many *rasas* have been evoked in this tragedy. There are many scenes in which there are only *bhāvas* and no *rasa.* Actually almost all the scenes in which Antony or Cleopatra do not appear fall flat. The only exception is Enobarbus's description. Even there Cleopatra, though physically absent, dominates the scene. It can be said with full justification that the rasa generated there is *adbhuta rasa*. It might be objected that this *rasa* depends on supernatural manifestation:

> *Atilaukaih padārthaih syād-vismayātmā raso-adbhutah.*[13]
>
> — The *adbhuta rasa* has for its soul the surprise generated by supernatural things.

It can be said that the description seems to be that of a beauty that has supernatural grace about it and this is heightened by repeated allusions to myths. The *Sañcārī bhavas* of this *rasa* are *sādhuvāda* (applause), *harṣa* (joy), *āvega* (deep feeling), etc. The two listeners Agrippa and Mecenas respond appropriately, exclaiming again and again "O rare for Antony" and the like. Cleopatra is the *ālambana* and Enobarbus and his two spellbound listeners are the *āśraya*. It can be said that Enobarbus is the *ālambana* but it seems to the present writer that that will not be correct. Cleopatra is so gloriously described as to be almost physically present. Enobarbus, through his memory, is as spellbound as his two listeners. The variety of *adbhutarasa* generated here is the *ānandaja* kind.

Even these few remarks show that the play is fully successful from the rasa point of view. A less cursory glance will show how many other rasas are generated that to support the *aṅgī rasa*.

REFERENCES

1. Sale, A., ed., *All for Love*, London, University Tutorial Press Ltd., n.d., pp. 16-17.
2. Brown, J.R. *op. cit.*, p. 26.
3. *Ibid.*, p. 29.
4. *Ibid.*, p. 43.
5. Spencer, T., *Shakespeare and the Nature of Man*, N.Y., The Macmillan Co., 1945, p. 163.
6. Brown, *op. cit.*, p. 121.
7. Dwivedi, Hazari Prasad and Dwivedi, Prithvinath, *Nāṭya Śastra Kī Paramparā aur Daśarūpaka*, New Delhi Rajkamal Prakashan, 1971, p. 67, I : II. When the original word is very long it has been split, with hyphens.

8. *Ibid.*, p. 167. 3 : 2.
9. *Ibid.*, p. 169. 3 : 33
10. V : ii : 359-60.
11. *Abhinava Bharati,* 1 : 292, Gaekwad Oriental Series, Baroda, n.d.
12. Dwivedi, *op.cit.*, 2 : 3.
13. *Ibid.*, 4 : 78.

A FEW IMPORTANT QUESTIONS

1. "*AC* shows both technical mastery and experimentation". Elucidate with examples.
2. "The conclusion of the play vindicates spiritual, not material values". Justify.
3. "In Antony we observe a mixture of great qualities, weaknesses and vices." Is this a true evaluation of Antony's character? Give reasons for your answer.
4. "As they die for each other, we forgive them for having lived for each other." Analyse the theme of love in the play in the light of this remark.
5. Hazlitt said, "The character of Cleopatra is a masterpiece". Do you agree? Give reasons for your answer.
6. Justify Coleridge's phrase "happy valiancy of style" with reference to *AC*.
7. Comment eritically on the remark that *AC* is "the finest of his historical plays".
8. Write a note on the imagery of *AC*.
9. Analyse the effect of the clown-scene in the last scene of *AC*.
10. Write a note on Shakespeare's use of Roman history in *AC*.

A SELECT BIBLIOGRAPHY

1. Bayley, John, *Shakespeare and Tragedy*, London, Routledge and Kegan Paul, 1981.
2. Bradrook, M.C. *Themes and Conventions in Elizabethan Tragedy*, Combr. University Press, 1935.
3. Bradley, *A.C. Shakespearean Tragedy*, London, Macmillan, 1960.
4. Bullough, G. *Narrative and Dramatic Sources of Shakespeare*, Vol. V, Lond., Routledge, 1966.
5. Clemen, W., *The Development of Shakespeare's Imagery*, Lond., Methuen, 1951.
6. Brown, J.R., ed., *Antony and Cleopatra: Casebook,* Lond., Macmillan, '1994 rpt.
7. Ribner, I., *Patterns in Shakespearean Tragedy*, Lond., Methuen, 1972.
8. Spencer, T., *Shakespeare and the Nature of Man*, N.Y., Macmillan, 1945.